BUILDING
NEW YORK

BUILDING NEW YORK

The Rise and Rise of the
Greatest City on Earth

Bruce Marshall

UNIVERSE

First published in the United States of America in 2005 by
UNIVERSE PUBLISHING
A Division of Rizzoli International Publications, Inc.
300 Park Avenue South
New York, NY 10010
www.rizzoli.com

Copyright © Getty Images, 2005

This book was produced by Getty Images
21–31 Woodfield Road
London W9 2BA
Fax 44 (020) 7266 2658

ISBN 0 - 7893 - 1362 - 6
Library of Congress Control Number: 2005928096

Managing Editor Mark Fletcher
Editor Sam Hudson
Proofreaders Nicky Gyopari and Liz Ihre
Picture Researcher Ali Khoja
Designer Paul Welti
Production Manager Mary Osborne

First Edition
2005 2006 2007 2008/10 9 8 7 6 5 4 3 2 1

Printed in Singapore

THE VALUE OF THE DOLLAR

*The cost of buildings is often mentioned in this book.
Here is an indication of what those sums mean in
today's terms:
$1 million of 1800 would be $14 million now.
Of 1850, $22 million. Of 1900, $20 million.
Of 1920, $9 million. Of 1940, $13 million.
Of 1950, $7.6 million. Of 1970, $4.7 million.*

*F.W. Woolworth paid $13.5 million – in cash –
for his eponymous building in 1913. That is
$250 million at 2003 values.*

*(Source: Political Science Department, Oregon
State University.)*

(PREVIOUS PAGES) *The Time & Life Building rises
as the city's tallest sheer-sided tower of its day. It is
across Sixth Avenue from the Rockefeller Center,
where media interests were always preferred tenants.*
HARRISON, ABRAMOVITZ & HARRIS, 1959

CONTENTS

INTRODUCTION

IT MUST HAVE BEEN ALL THE TELEVISION in my childhood; I really can't get through a history of New York without pictures. To me, the richest and most creative accounts of the development of the city – like I. N. Phelps Stokes' *Iconography of Manhattan Island* and John Atlee Kouwenhoven's *Columbia Historical Portrait of New York* – are conceived specifically for photographs. There is something about a picture which gives much greater resonance to 10, 100, or 1,000 words – and this is true with those Bruce Marshall has incorporated into *Building New York*.

Take the frontispiece, the topping out of the Time & Life building, at Sixth Avenue and 50th Street. It captures the sky-breaking insolence of the new, reductionist office buildings of the 1950s and 1960s just as well as even the tersest ridicule by Ada Louise Huxtable, architecture critic for the *New York Times*. And yet it also shows them as part of the native growth of the city, towering over the ancient side streets' rowhouses and tenements – considered then to be the source of blight; it shows the parking lots made ready to receive the new towers by the clearing of the same side streets, and temporarily taken up by the automobiles in full swarm over the city; it shows the irrelevance of the older architecture – even Rockefeller Center – in the face of the new corporate demand for broad office floors; and it shows even this epoch of the city as the product of human endeavor: the six workmen on the roof, looking out at the camera and towards the crazy photographer suspended out over 40 floors of nothingness.

I always prefer the hypnotic time-transfer of a sharp photograph – even if the camera image often does lie – but still, the crude early views, like the early engraving of "Nieuw Amsterdam," can sometimes provide the same transport to an earlier era. The raw, innocent shoreline, with its tideline of rocks; the windmill – did windmills really spin over the island? – and, front and center, the gibbet. The city's cup of sin is still over-full.

The big city is too big to be captured by one story line. New York is not a rainbow coalition but a pile of broken glass, each piece glinting in a different direction. That's why Mr. Marshall's episodic approach is much more readable than a continuous narrative, which often forces the author and reader into a single argument, like a debate conclusion, as if any city was a single thing. Rather *Building New York* yields an ambling journey, like the braided channels of an ancient river delta.

The pictures Mr. Marshall has chosen, especially the photographs, are best when they show the city as a completely human endeavor, the product of individual wills and hands, built for the quotidian use of its citizens. For this reason traditional architectural history – which almost always treats with the easy arcana of architectural style and form – deadens the quick-beating life of New York, where "architecture" embraces loan rates, building laws, union power, jealousy, incompetence, dollars per square foot and other down and dirty realities.

Thus the smoky, sun-rayed interior of Grand Central on page 35, with shadowy rail passengers caught in ballet on the terminal floor, catches the experience of the building much more effectively than the usual architectural photograph. And it is the workers, almost invisible in the devastated landscape of the excavation of Penn Station on pages 40–41, that give the photograph scale and life.

With the best of these images there is a resonance between the architectural and the human condition, as with the single surviving rowhouse on East 68th Street on page 167, its jagged walls protesting its own imminent passing, with the like-proportioned human figures – man, woman, child – passing it by on the sidewalk. And such documentary photographs are often artful without necessarily being art: in the construction scene on the Bank of the Manhattan Company each man in the riveting crew echoes in some way the peculiar parallelogram of the planks below them.

These photographs can also capture the warp and woof of the city, things which are often unexpressed (or at least invisible) in traditional accounts: the wind on page 56; the human necessities of a house on page 268; the growing baggage of street signage in the auto age, cluttering the cityscape in a perversely inverse proportion to the modernist simplification of the city, on page 187. The purist Le Corbusier would never have allowed it – but then he didn't design from ground level.

Can anything explain the clack-clack-clack of the almost extinct elevated railroads better than the photographs on pages 46–51? And then there are the happy collisions of intention and chance, like the photograph of the Museum of Modern Art on page 188. Was the photographer there to portray New York's ultra-serious bastion of modern art? If so, how fortune smiled, with a skywriter working on a canvas far bigger than anything inside!

These things – the incidental, the accidental, the unplanned – are the ones that convey most faithfully the constant juxtaposition of human life in New York, something rarely seen in traditional history. *Building New York* captures not only the facts, but also the feeling.

CHRISTOPHER GRAY

PROLOGUE

T‍HE FIRST IMAGES of the settlement that was to become New York show a cluster of church steeples, patches of tulips among the bark huts, canals, and windmills. But such ordered Dutch daintiness was not to last. By 1643 a Jesuit missionary was reporting a babble of languages (he identified 18), corruption, random violence, and drunkenness – one in four buildings, he said, was a tavern.

Among the three burgeoning cities of the north-east, New York was the rowdy, the wild one. Puritan principles kept the lid on Boston and William Penn's Quakers fiercely preserved Philadelphia's morals. But New York had no such disciplines. Opportunism and exploitation, wealth and misery overlaid its progress right from its founding.

The attraction for the rich, the would-be rich, and the toiling poor was the port, the most protected on the Atlantic seaboard, with the Hudson River offering a trade route into the continent. The English explorer Henry Hudson recognized and

A trading post takes shape on the southern tip of the island. This was truly a company town: the first European settlers, 30 families, were posted here by the Dutch West India Company to exploit the fur trade. They built a brewery before they built a church.

NIEUW AMSTERDAM
op t Eylant Manhattans.

reported the potential, but it was Dutch fur traders who planted the flag and bought the island of Manna-Hattan for beads from the resident Native Americans, who could have had no idea of the concept of trade across an ocean. A defensive redoubt was built along the line of present-day Wall Street; it kept marauding natives at bay, but not the English, who came by sea to seize the colony in the name of the Duke of York in 1664.

By 1790, New York was the largest city in the United States and, briefly, the Federal capital. On the waterfront, shipwrights were not averse to servicing the pirate ships that preyed on coastal traffic. John Jacob Astor landed a shipload of Chinese porcelain, silk, and spices to make his first fortune. A decade later the population had doubled, to 60,000; a century later it was 1 million.

The grand plans were set as the 19th century began. A stock exchange was established, Alexander Hamilton founded the Bank of New York, and work began on City Hall, which is still in use. The Erie Canal (1825) linked with the Hudson River to complete a waterway to Albany, Buffalo, and the Great Lakes. The transit of grain and meat from the Midwest made New York the nation's principal seaboard gateway, and soon it would have the biggest railroad terminal on the Atlantic coast.

The signature grid plan was authorized in 1811, an old idea recently revived by the city's arch-rival, Philadelphia, where Penn had applied it to simplify the mechanics of selling land

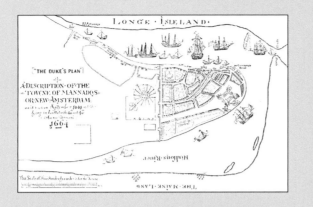

"The Duke's Plan" of 1664 outlines the Duke of York's new property. Already there is a "suburb" north-east of the rampart that would become Wall Street, alongside a quay for the ferry to Brooklyn. The ships fly English flags, but the colony has not yet been renamed.

plots. While the road on the old hunting trail, now called Broadway, would continue to meander the length of the island, wide north–south avenues were to anchor a rigidly rectangular pattern of cross streets marching from shore to shore. However, passage from South Street, "the street of ships," on the East River, to the deeper water anchorages on the Hudson would continue to be hampered by the haphazard footprint of the old settlement.

As the roadbuilders cut their swathes northward, Astor and his friends decided that Fifth Avenue was the place to be and began building mansions there. Meanwhile, racial turf wars, exploitation and corruption, crime, yellow fever, and cholera blighted the lives of the migrants bottom-feeding in this cauldron of opportunity. Their slums on the Lower East Side, below 14th Street, between Broadway and the East River, were reckoned to be the most densely packed area in the world –

The most devastating fire in the city's history was recorded by the artist Nicolino Calyo (LEFT), whose gouache paintings became best-selling engravings. For two days in the winter of 1835, the blaze raged through the wooden buildings of the Lower East Side.

PROSPERITY FLOWS FROM "THE BIG DITCH"

The first of the many impossible dreams that came true for New York was the Erie Canal, a waterway carved through mountains and wilderness to connect the Hudson River to the heart of the continent – below in a watercolour from 1829.

The dreamer was De Witt Clinton, at various times a U.S. Senator, mayor of the city, and governor of the state. Refused Federal funding – Thomas Jefferson told him that it was a project for "a century hence" – Clinton issued bonds backed by a state salt tax. Work began in July 1817. Mostly wielding picks and shovels, 9,000 men dug out "Clinton's Big Ditch," 360 miles long, from Buffalo to Albany, 40 ft. wide and 12 ft. deep.

Learning canal-building as they went along – it was an enterprise without precedent, the most ambitious construction of its time – they built 83 locks and 18 aqueducts. When Clinton ceremonially poured a bucket of Lake Erie water into New York Harbor three years ahead of the 10-year schedule, he could tell his investors that the project was within its $6 million budget.

Now the port of New York linked with the trade routes of the St. Lawrence and the Mississippi. Cotton and grain, meat and minerals loaded at the Great Lakes reached the Atlantic seaboard in seven days rather than three weeks. New York was unassailably the country's commercial capital.

THE GRID PLAN

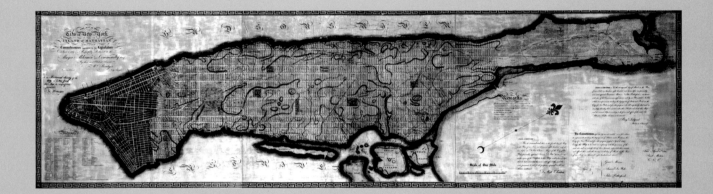

The city's northern limit was Canal Street when John Randel was commissioned to survey the rest of the island. His team hacked their way through a wilderness of woodland, over hills and rocky outcrops, across streams, ponds, and marshes, challenged by suspicious squatters and smallholders who lived off the better bits of land. When the Commissioners' Plan for development was published in 1811, it ignored the topography of Manhattan. "These are men who would have cut down the seven hills of Rome," one critic said.

The landscape would be flattened, inconvenient hills being shoveled into inconvenient swamps, and all would be overlaid with a rigid pattern of 100-ft. wide north–south avenues and 155 cross streets set at 200-ft. intervals. The old native trail that starts at the Battery, Broadway, interrupts the gridiron, but, at this stage, there is no sign of Central Park. The planners considered that as everyone on the island was within a mile of the rivers, waterfronts would be the city's breathing spaces. But port facilities, railroad tracks, and highways soon blocked them

John Randel did the survey work and drew a meticulous map. He was outraged when the name printed largest on the published version was "Wm. Bridges." Bridges, officially the city surveyor, but no cartographer, had traced it, and effectively stolen the copyright. He sold copies of the 8-ft.-long sheet for up to $15.50.

off, and Broadway's diagonal meandering, inconvenient to the block-minded developers, left spaces that would be important to the city – Times Square and Union Square, for instance.

As a planning model, the grid has a long history. Labor camps for Egypt's pyramid builders were laid out in this way, and later Greek and Roman colonies used it, often orientating the main streets to the sunrise. The checkerboard pattern gave clear lines of sight for early warning of marauders from land and sea, it eased the movement of defenders and their equipment, and allowed breezes to ventilate narrow streets. Local precedents for New York's use of it came from Philadelphia, Savannah, Charleston, and New Orleans.

The 1830s home of the Society of St. Tammany (ABOVE) whose political machine soon became notoriously corrupt. The first presidential mansion was on Cherry Street (ABOVE RIGHT). George Washington lived there briefly in 1789, when New York was the nation's capital.

The ports are alive with commerce in 1853 (BELOW). The northward expansion of Manhattan is well under way, but church steeples still dominate the skyline.

600 residents to the acre in the worst of the tenement blocks at the peak of the compression. Charles Dickens reported in shocked terms to his London readers that scavenging pigs roamed Broadway.

Fire after fire after fire ravaged the wooden hovels. But the quarries of Connecticut and New Jersey were opening up. Granite and sandstone, clay for bricks, and the ingredients for cement could be shipped down Long Island Sound into the East River and across the bay from Jersey. The new slums could be more permanent – stable if wretched homes for the workforce who would build the city, creating the most completely man-made environment on earth, "squeezing profit out of every inch of the dirt beneath their feet."

The last of the salt marshes south of Wall Street were filled. Urban development overwhelmed the woods and streams of middle Manhattan and the meadows and farmlands in Harlem.

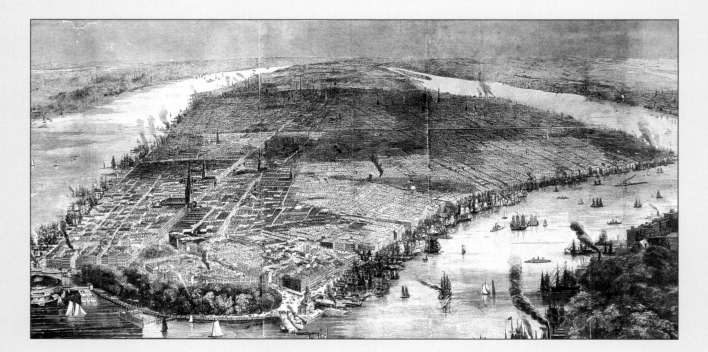

STATUE OF LIBERTY

Torch-bearer for New York

SCULPTOR
Frédéric-Auguste Bartholdi

COMPLETED
1886

A CURIOUS MONUMENT, one that frightened the children, appeared on the west side of Madison Square in the 1870s: the amputated hand of a woman, in copper, with an 8-ft. high index finger steadying a torch. It was a section of the 150-ft. tall statue the French nation wished to present to the American people, placed on this Fifth Avenue corner to encourage more gracious appreciation among New Yorkers. It would mark the gateway to New York harbor — if only the city would pay for the pedestal. But New York wouldn't. In the depression following the financial crash of 1873, official opinion was that this was not a proper use of public money.

This was the second time the Lady had been spurned. The French sculptor Frédéric-Auguste Bartholdi had originally planned

the figure as a symbolic lighthouse to mark the entrance to the Suez Canal. But the Khedive of Egypt balked at the cost. Now, in New York, it took several years of private fund-raising, and nickels and dimes contributed by readers of Joseph Pulitzer's *World* newspaper, to get the base on Bedloe's Island built and the Statue of Liberty out of its packing cases.

Architect Gustave Eiffel, whose own masterwork was still to be built in Paris, worked on the iron internal structure, making it flexible enough to withstand the harbor's gales and allowing for a 168-step staircase inside the gown of hand-hammered copper plates.

On October 28, 1886, the gift the French had been trying to give New York for 20 years was dedicated by President Cleveland. Over the next 30 years it would be the first sight of America for 20 million immigrants arriving at Ellis Island.

The Lady's hand gestured for attention at the Philadelphia centennial exhibition in 1876. Then it appeared in Madison Square Park (ABOVE). It would eventually be 300 ft. above sea level when the statue was anchored to its 142-ft.-high granite and concrete base.

Head and shoulders above Paris in 1878, where the citizens could admire the gift they were paying for through public subscription. They were also charged 50 centimes to climb the stairs into the spiked crown.

ELLIS ISLAND

Gateway to the promised land

ARCHITECT
Boring & Tilton

COMPLETED
1900

THE FIRST WAVES OF IMMIGRANTS stepped ashore at Castle Garden, Battery Park – more than 7 million of them between 1855 and 1890. As the numbers grew, a more dedicated facility, less disruptive to Manhattan life, was required. Ellis Island, in sight of the Statue of Liberty, was chosen as the landfall for the world's weary. Dutch colonists had picnicked there, pirates had been hanged, then it was an ammunition dump whose explosive potential dismayed the residents of nearby New Jersey.

Wooden buildings occupied the three-acre island when it welcomed its first migrants in 1892. After a fire in 1897, a brick-and-concrete facility took shape. The planners expected half a million new-comers a year; in 1907 it was double that number. Ellis Island grew to 27 acres, created by landfill, and became a complex of hearings rooms, dormitories, laundry, dining hall, kindergarten, hospital, quarantine wards, and guarded rooms for dangerous deportees. It closed in 1954.

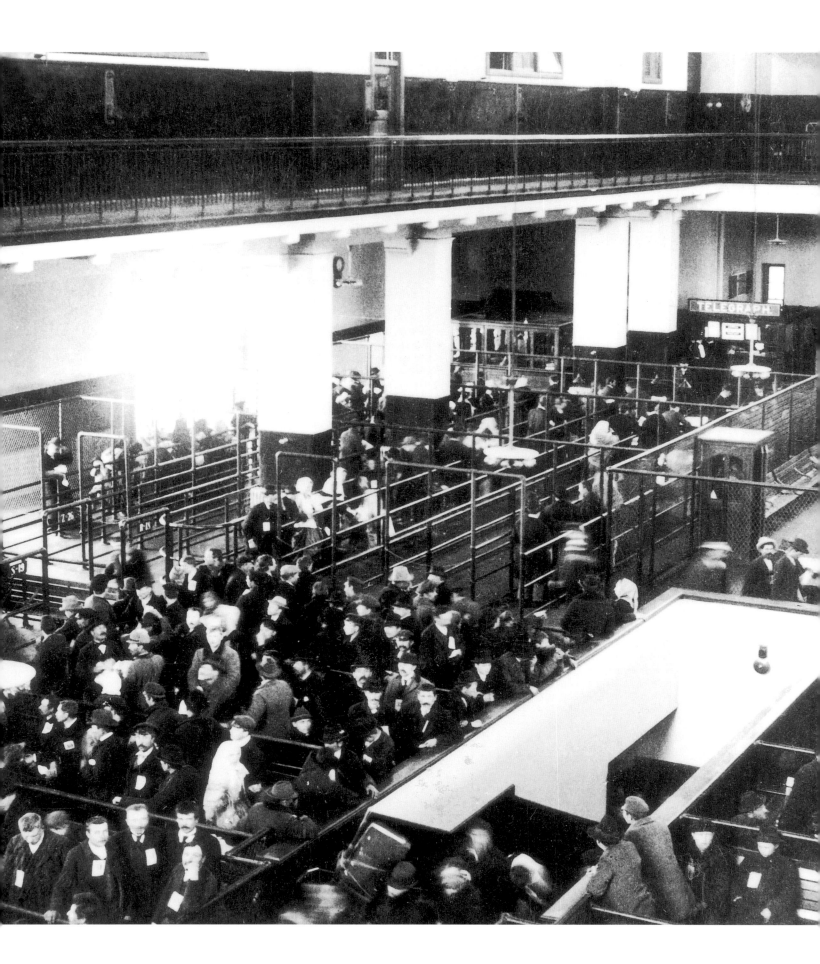

On deck for the welcoming lady (LEFT) *circa 1915. In the Registry Room* (ABOVE)
*hopefuls await the fateful tests and interviews. Inspectors could deny entry for some
60 reasons, most of them medical, but they were also on the lookout for polygamists
and paupers, anarchists and the criminally insane. Only steerage passengers were
made to pass through Ellis Island. First- and second-class travelers were waved
through cursory controls at the Hudson River port. The island's principal buildings
have been restored as a museum of immigration.*

BROOKLYN BRIDGE

Eighth Wonder of the World

CHIEF ENGINEER
John Augustus Roebling

COMPLETED
1883

IN THE MID-19TH CENTURY, it seemed that the future of New York might lay in Brooklyn, already the third-largest city in the United States. Growth was finite on Manhattan island: city blocks, the 2,000 pre-ordained by the grid plan, were rapidly filling up, mostly with buildings no higher than four stories, the practical maximum at the time. Brooklyn, on the other hand, could spread – all of Long Island was at its doorstep. Some planners wistfully looked to two classical examples of metropolitan growth where the same

geographical conditions applied: London and Paris, great cities spreading on both sides of great rivers.

Certainly, ferry traffic across the East River – 100,000 passengers a day by the 1870s – indicated the bond between Brooklyn and Manhattan. But the river was subject to the tyrannies of the weather, and it was aboard an East River ferry blocked by winter iceflows that engineer John Augustus Roebling resolved to build a bridge – one giant leap, one great arch across the world's busiest waterway.

If anybody could do it, Roebling could. As an engineering student in Berlin, he had mastered the theories of bridge building. As a migrant to the United States he had built suspension bridges across the Niagara Falls and the Ohio River. In New Jersey he had made a fortune manufacturing iron wire cable as a stronger, more durable alternative to hemp rope; now there was steel cable, the crucial element of the design he submitted for one of the most ambitious engineering projects of the 19th century. From two great towers, a 1,600-ft. span would be suspended 130 ft. above mean high water – twice the distance so far accomplished.

It took Roebling 10 years to convince the skeptics, override the vested interests of the ferry lines, raise the finances, and form the New York Bridge Company. But no sooner had work begun, in 1869, than its pioneer was gone. On a site visit, Roebling suffered a crushed foot as a ferryboat crumpled the wooden pier on which he was standing. Tetanus and lockjaw followed emergency surgery, and

Newly recruited workers were required to prove their head for heights by walking the suspension cable where these supervisors nonchalantly pose (LEFT). To make the cables, 15,000 miles of steel wire were looped back and forth across the river and then bound into bundles 16 inches in diameter.

The city's proudest project lit for a party in 1909 (ABOVE) – this one honoring the city's other river. The Hudson–Fulton Celebration marked the 300th anniversary of Henry Hudson's cruise into the river that he named for himself; Robert Fulton built the first steamboat to carry passengers on the Hudson.

John Augustus Roebling died just as work began on his elegantly over-engineered design. It was later calculated that the structure was capable of bearing the weight of the Empire State Building's steel carcass – 60,000 tons.

he died within days. His son, Washington Roebling, a U.S. Army engineer, took command.

The younger Roebling was himself to be a victim of the project. Building the granite suspension towers required foundations set on the river's bedrock. Huge, bottomless wooden boxes, caissons, were lowered into the water, and workers inside, breathing pumped-in air, dug out the riverbed mud. A strange, debilitating sickness afflicted the men, and even at wages of $2.25 a day – the highest laboring rate in the city – turnover was high. The problem was caisson disease, later known as decompression sickness, or the bends. Roebling himself, a hands-on supervisor, was stricken in 1872 and thereafter directed progress from his bedroom in Brooklyn, with a telescope at the window and his wife, Emily, as liaison officer.

The caissons were filled with cement, granite blocks were shipped down Long Island Sound from Maine, and in 1876 residents of the two cities looked in wonder at the two double-arched Gothic towers, the most massive man-made structures on the continent, with only the slender spire of nearby Trinity Church higher on the city's skyline.

Four catenaries, the main suspension cables across the divide, were made of spliced steel wire to be wrapped in situ in yet more

The Brooklyn caisson is readied (BELOW). Working inside this wooden box, breathing pumped-in air, men known as "sandhogs" dug out the river bed until the caisson rested on bedrock. Then it was filled with concrete to take the granite base of a tower (ABOVE) on which a mighty gothic arch would be erected.

wire. (Among the examples of the endemic corruption that plagued the project was the supply of defective wire that Roebling, in his bedroom, could snap between his fingers. Emily Roebling's capabilities in such situations in a community of hard men were later in her life to be put to doughty use in the campaign for women's rights.) More steel cables, verticals, and diagonals supported the bridge deck, an avenue as wide as Broadway. A footbridge gave strollers the first experience of a city rising into the sky.

Finally, in 1883, nine years later than John Roebling had scheduled and costing more than twice his budget, with a death toll of almost 30 and many more invalided by the bends, "the eighth wonder of the world" opened. The date chosen for the ceremony was May 24, Queen Victoria's birthday, an affront to the Irish who had given labor and lives to the project. After the greatest fireworks display in the city's history, the lights were switched on, energized by Thomas Edison's new power station on Pearl Street.

With that light show, the two base elements of the rise of their city were on view to New Yorkers: steel for the skeletons of their skyscrapers, and electricity to drive the elevators.

The Brooklyn approach to the bridge after a blizzard in 1888 (ABOVE). The roadway platform is 86 ft. wide, with outer lanes for horse-drawn traffic. The central 12-ft.-wide boardwalk had elevated cable railroad tracks on either side. Later, the bridge was adapted to take six lanes of highway.

This is a quiet day on the bridge's central walkway (RIGHT) in a photograph taken a few days after a panic exodus in 1883 caused the deaths of 12 pedestrians; thus the calming presence of a policeman. But the bridge offered Sunday sightseers views of the East River, the port, and downtown Manhattan from the highest man-made promenade in the world.

Atop the towers (LEFT), the four suspension cables, each made up of 24,000 steel wires, are carried on saddles, in turn resting on beds of steel rollers. Landfall on the Jersey side is at Fort Lee; in Manhattan, at 179th Street.

Tunnels were blasted into the Palisades rock to take the bridge's New Jersey anchorage (RIGHT). On the Manhattan side, a huge concrete block in Fort Washington Park takes the strain. The two moorings are almost a mile apart.

GEORGE WASHINGTON BRIDGE

New York to New Jersey

ENGINEER
Othmar Hermann Ammann

COMPLETED
1931

THE "MOST SPLENDID OF NEW YORK'S BRIDGES" is the city's only visible connection to New Jersey. Until San Francisco built its two great bridges, it was the world's longest suspension span, 3,500 ft. of it, twice as long as anything before, suspended more than 200 ft. above the Hudson River from four 4 ft. diameter cables.

The most admired feature of the design, its signature, is the pair of graceful, arched steel towers, topping out 600 ft. above the Hudson. In fact, the intention was to sheathe them in granite, but the Depression caused a cut in the budget. The Port of New York Authority had conceived the bridge as a railroad link. Then road traffic lanes were added to the design. But even before work began, the case for the automobile had become overwhelming and the bridge was built to take only roadways. By 1938, it was earning $5 million a year in tolls, almost 10 percent of its cost. The original stress calculations allowed for the addition of a second, lower deck, which was completed in 1962, and with that in place, the George Washington Bridge became a crucial connector; in transportation terms, Manhattan was no longer an island.

The Port Authority commissioned the Italian architect-engineer Pier Luigi Nervi to build a boldly conceived uptown bus terminal that fed directly into the bridge, serving hordes of New Jersey commuters. There was now a smooth approach to the interstate highways heading west. Soon, the bridge linked to a 12-lane expressway cutting across Manhattan, coiling interchanges led to parkways, driveways, and a new span across the Harlem River.

"The George Washington Bridge is the most beautiful bridge in the world …. It is blessed. It is the only seat of grace in the disordered city."

LE CORBUSIER, architect

THE EAST RIVER BRIDGES

Untroubled by the waters

ONCE THE BROOKLYN BRIDGE had paved the way out of Manhattan, bridge-building became a city obsession. Bonding the five boroughs into greater New York would, in time, lead to more than 70 bridges over the region's waterways. In the 20 years around the turn of the 20th century, eight spans were built across the Harlem River, the frontier to the north, and three more arched over the East River.

The first of those was the Williamsburg (1903), the longest, heaviest, and ugliest, suspension bridge of its day, with a 1,600-ft. span carrying traffic lanes, railroad tracks, and sidewalks between Delancey Street on the Lower East Side and the affluent neighborhood of Williamsburg. The social effect, a portent of the unrest to come when Robert Moses realigned the city's communities, was an influx of poor immigrants from the Lower East Side. In 20 years, Williamsburg's population more than doubled, and tenement blocks replaced gracious brownstones.

Six years later, the Manhattan Bridge offered seven vehicle lanes and four subway tracks for Brooklyn traffic. Perhaps mindful of the aesthetic criticism of the Williamsburg Bridge, the architects built an arch on the

Lattice curtains of steel
trusses give the Williamsburg
Bridge (ABOVE LEFT) great
strength and its "graceless"
appearance.

The 1,470-ft. main span
of the Manhattan Bridge
(ABOVE) clears the East
River by 135 ft. When the
Holland Tunnel was
bored from the other, western,
end of Canal Street, the
bridge's two levels were
heavily used by New
Jersey–Long Island traffic.

On a wintry day in 1908,
the Queensboro's cantilever
reaches across the East River
(BELOW LEFT).

The longest steel arch of
its time nears completion
at the Hell Gate Bridge
(BELOW RIGHT).

Canal Street approach in a style suggesting one of the gateways to Paris.

In the same year, 1909, the Queensboro Bridge, better known to locals as the 59th Street Bridge, reached Long Island City by way of a step on Welfare Island, later named Roosevelt Island. A cantilevered construction, it was the first major New York bridge not to use the suspension system. It, too, transformed its landfall: by 1930 the population of Queens had quadrupled, the assessed value of its properties had increased sixfold.

Hell Gate is the name of a narrow channel between Astoria and Ward's Island, whose underwater rocks and vicious currents had doomed many earlier seafarers. The span that stepped over it in 1917 completed a continuous, direct railroad route from Maine to Miami, a service New Yorkers could reach from Penn Station.

And soon it was Robert Moses's turn, building the bridges carrying the highways that would finally eradicate the notion that the city was an island (technically, only the Bronx is on the mainland). Among them were the Throgs Neck Bridge, the Bronx–Whitestone, the Henry Hudson, and, most remarkably, the Triborough and the Verrazano Narrows bridges.

The main span of the Triborough is
hoisted into position (ABOVE). Two
of the bridge's spans had lift
mechanisms to permit the passage
of large ships. The Triborough was
considered to have "the most ingenious
traffic-sorter ever constructed" (RIGHT).
But, inevitably, the bridge encouraged new
road users who experienced a new
phenomenon – traffic jams as they slowed
for the exits. Robert Moses's response was
to build the Bronx–Whitestone Bridge.

TRIBOROUGH BRIDGE

Heading for the beaches

WORK BEGAN, AND STOPPED, on the Triborough as the stock market crashed in 1929. Resuming in 1933, contractors on "the most ambitious transportation project of the age" linked Manhattan, Queens, and the Bronx by way of stepping stones on Randall's and Ward islands. Four overwater spans and 12 over land amounted to an elevated length of almost three and a half miles in an overall complex of swirling under- and overpasses and highway connections stretching for 14 miles. At the eastern end, New Yorkers were finally on prettified parkways to the Long Island recreation areas Robert Moses had built for them.

The Triborough was the core of Moses's plan for an auto-based metropolis, and the prime example of his ruthless energy. He spent $60 million on the project. He brought 600 unemployed architects and engineers back into service. At any one time, the construction force would be 5,000 strong. An entire Oregon forest was felled to make forms for concrete. All over the country, cement factories and steel mills, idle due to the Depression, were reopened.

In the shadows of the new constructions, parks and playgrounds were landscaped. Astoria gained a massive outdoor swimming pool; Randall's Island, a municipal stadium. And Moses took the opportunity to build himself a new headquarters, significantly right below the toll booths. Now adding "Chairman of the Triborough Bridge Authority" to his several public works and parks titles, he had the cash cow that would underwrite future projects. In its first full year, 1937, the bridge generated $2.7 million in tolls, opening an account that would fund his restructuring of the city.

ARCHITECT
Aymar Embury II

ENGINEER
Othmar Hermann Ammann

COMPLETED
1936

VERRAZANO NARROWS BRIDGE

Framing the nation's front door

DESIGNER
Othmar Hermann Ammann

COMPLETED
1964, Lower deck, 1969

GIOVANNI DA VERRAZANO was the first European to sail into New York's territorial waters. Robert Moses spanned the Narrows named for him, the entrance to the Upper Bay, with another bravura project, completed in 1964. To the dismay of some of its isolationist citizens, Staten Island now had physical attachment to its fellow metropolitan boroughs.

Framing "the front door to the nation" required the longest suspension span of its day — at 4,260 ft. it took the record back from San Francisco's Golden Gate. It is an arch so long that the 690-ft. towers supporting it are farther apart at the top than at the bottom due to the earth's curvature.

The towers sit on steel and concrete foundations plugged into islands of sand. Behind them, at Fort Hamilton in Brooklyn and Fort Wadsworth on Staten Island, huge concrete blocks anchor four steel wire suspension cables, each three ft. in diameter. The two levels of roadway they support carry 12 lanes of highway.

The human cost of the project was the displacement of 8,000 residents of Bay Ridge, the Brooklyn terminus of a facility that is, overall, 2.6 miles long. Among the beneficiaries were New Jersey's travelers who now had a short cut to JFK Airport and Long Island.

GRAND CENTRAL TERMINAL

The city's spectacular gateway

ARCHITECTS
Reed & Stem, Warren & Wetmore

COMPLETED
1913

THERE WAS A TIME when a journey by train was considered a glamorous adventure: it was as good to travel as to arrive, like flying by Clipper in the 1940s. Men wore ties and their best suits; ladies donned hats and gloves. Grand Central opened in 1913, to symbolize that era, and Manhattan's pride of place in it. There's no question, the styling stated, that to arrive here is to arrive at the capital of the known universe.

The severely formal façade on 42nd Street, a Beaux-Arts triumph, is pierced by vaulted arches illuminating a stately concourse, walled in marble, with glamorous balconies, sweeping staircases, gracious waiting rooms, and a huge iron clock counting the minutes of an unrelenting

Grand Central Depot was the earlier terminal on the site (ABOVE). It was a conceit of Commodore Vanderbilt to put "central" in the name: the depot was way to the north of the working city when it opened in 1871. The train shed was the largest covered space on the continent. Smoke and steam rose to a 100-ft.-high iron and glass ceiling.

The terminal was just two years old when these travelers admired the cathedral-like lighting of the concourse (RIGHT). There are no trains at this level; ramps lead passengers to the underground tracks.

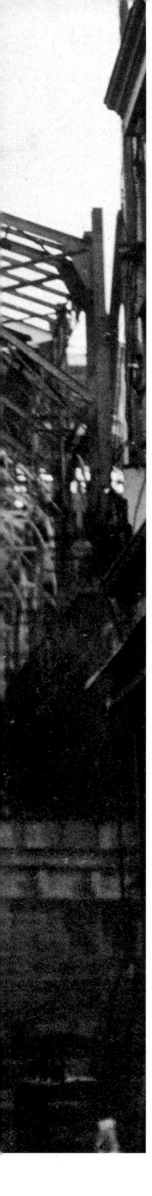

schedule. And there's not a train in sight; they are discreetly hidden underground.

There is railroad history here older than the building. The site had been Grand Central Depot, built by Cornelius Vanderbilt as the terminus for his Hudson River and New York Central Railroads. By the turn of the 20th century this vast, sooty train yard was considered "a disgrace to the metropolis."

As New York developers began to reach for the sky, the Vanderbilts' chief engineer, William J. Wilgus, looked the other way. His new terminal would burrow down. On two levels underground there would be almost 80 acres of train yard, 100 tracks, stretching from Madison Avenue to Lexington Avenue and north to 56th Street. The locomotives would use the new clean electrical power; a loop track would eliminate the need for switching and shunting space to get them pointed in the right directions. Furthermore, if the heart of Wilgus's "Terminal City" could be a low building, there would be air rights to sell to the hotel developers who would surely appear to serve the travelers. The 1,000-room Biltmore quickly proved the point.

Grand Central welcomed transcontinental voyagers, commuters, and fashionable locals. The balconies and staircases became places to promenade on the way to a newsreel cinema, an art gallery, and smart restaurants. But it was not to last. Long-distance travelers turned to the airlines, commuters took to the roads, Penn Station competed for the fewer railroad

The barrel-vaulting of the concourse takes shape. Grand Central took 10 years to build, and throughout that time train services continued, using the old Grand Central Depot. Most of the tracks were routed along what is now Park Avenue. As traffic declined after World War II, the station's owners and commercial developers regularly advanced plans to build several stories into the vast, 125-ft.-high space of the Main Concourse. But it was given landmark status, which thwarted such plans.

A $200 million restoration in the 1990s reopened a long-blocked hallway revealing Beaux Arts details. The main façade, facing south on 42nd Street, features three monumental arches in the manner of a classical city gateway. It was here that the smartest crowd of the day would alight to take the 6PM Twentieth Century Limited to Chicago, their passage eased by some of the station's 500 red-capped porters.

passengers, and, by the 1960s, Grand Central was a sad, dirty place, a home for vagrants and raucous billboards.

The Committee to Save Grand Central was formed, with Jacqueline Kennedy Onassis among its founders. Several plans to build over and smother the original building were thwarted. Concourse advertisements were removed. The patina was restored to marble and metal was burnished. The barrel-vaulted ceiling was cleaned to reveal a long-forgotten mural of the Milky Way. Glory returned to what the architect Philip Johnson called "the greatest room in New York."

A massive statuary group by Jules Couton tops the 42nd Street façade. Over a clock 13 ft. across, Mercury, the god of travel and commerce, has the backing of the American Eagle as he greets travelers. To his right, Hercules signifies strength and courage; Minerva, on his left, the patron of arts and crafts, acknowledges the skills that created the great building below her. A classical association the Vanderbilts may not have recognized is that in Roman mythology, Mercury also symbolized thievery.

GRAND CENTRAL
TERMINAL

PENNSYLVANIA STATION

Doomed shrine of the railroad age

ARCHITECTS
McKim, Mead & White

COMPLETED
1911

BEFORE PENN STATION, the final stage of a railroad journey from the south or west was a ferry ride across the Hudson from New Jersey. But as the 20th century dawned, tunnel-boring technology was up to the challenge of carrying track under the river, and electrification nullified the problem of smoke-filled tubes. The Pennsylvania Railroad Company could contemplate building a terminal in Manhattan.

The result was "the largest, handsomest railroad station in the world." The architects' inspiration was Roman Classicism, in particular the Baths of Caracalla in Rome. A long, barrel-vaulted

In 1906, eight acres are cleared and excavated (ABOVE) to take two levels of underground tracks and underpin an instantly-famous building. The granite exterior (OVERLEAF) clad a steel frame built on 650 steel foundation columns. Here at the corner of Seventh Avenue is one of the colonnaded end pavilions with access for motor vehicles – an early understanding of the city's impending traffic congestion. This frontage extended across two city blocks. Sixty years later the site would be cleared again, to make way for the entertainment complex, Madison Square Garden.

entrance lobby and marble stairs led to a vast hall decorated with murals of the railroads' destinations. A huge glass-roofed concourse gave access to the tracks of the Pennsylvania's services, and those of the Long Island Railroad, which had tunneled under the East River. A connection over the Hell Gate Bridge allowed trains to run all the way from Maine to Miami.

But by the 1960s, travelers to Philadelphia and beyond were more likely to fly; Long Island commuters were crowding the Long Island Expressway. Despite angry public protest, the financially troubled Pennsylvania Railroad Company brought in the wreckers, and the station infrastructure went underground. Sixty years after the finest

Penn Station's interior facings were largely of travertine marble, an extravagant import, but it was the vastness of two central spaces that really awed the visitor. The ceiling of the main waiting room, Roman-inspired, was coffered and seemingly supported by

Corinthian columns (LEFT); *100 ft. above the concourse, a glass roof rested on steel vaulting* (ABOVE). *Nearby on Eighth Avenue, the station's architects, McKim, Mead & White, built another important formal building, the New York General Post Office.*

landmark of the age of the train took its proud place between Seventh and Eighth Avenues, at 31st and 33rd Streets, it was demolished. Just four stories high, one of the last remaining grandly horizontal buildings, it had air rights too valuable for its owners to ignore. One commentator mourning the passing of an American treasure said, "Through it one entered the city like a god … now, one scuttles in like a rat."

The massive classical columns, the granite angels and carved eagles that adorned Penn Station were dumped into a New Jersey swamp. One consoling outcome of the demolition was the founding of the city's 1965 Landmarks Preservation Commission.

THE EL

Going to work on stilts

FIRST CONSTRUCTOR
Charles Harvey, the West Side
and Yonkers Patent Railway

COMPLETED
1867–70

NEW YORK WAS AMONG A FEW American cities that made an eccentric decision about the style of their urban railroad systems. Paris, London, and Moscow would hide theirs underground, hardly disturbing traffic on the streets, but Manhattan built its first network on stilts — the El (for "elevated"), which would disfigure Second, Third, Sixth, and Ninth Avenues for the better part of a century.

In the mid-19th century, the stone underpinning of the city seemed a formidable obstacle to tunneling, and the railroad barons, powerful enough to corrupt and override the public interest, looked to make the most profit from the least capital expenditure. Overground was cheaper than underground. Exotic ideas were proposed, and discarded: overhead viaducts for horse-drawn omnibuses,

Demonstrating a cable-hauled car in
1867 (ABOVE LEFT) . The line was
to run from the Battery to Yonkers,
north of the city. But its finances failed
at 31st Street. Under this junction
lies Chatham Square (ABOVE).
The earliest locomotives wore shrouds
to disperse smoke and muffle noise –

so as not to frighten the horses.
Roofs of rails are still in place in these
1946 photographs (OVERLEAF LEFT).
The El brought perpetual twilight to
the wide avenues that framed the city's
grid plan, allowing just a dappling of
sunlight here under the Third Avenue
El at 34th Street (OVERLEAF RIGHT).

The Big S at Coenties Slip (ABOVE), where the Third Avenue El reached the end of the line, the harbor in the background. An artists' community took over the area when this section of track was demolished. In the 1970s, that made way for the world's largest commercial office building.

El passengers had close-up views of every setting for city life, from the trim suburbs of the outer boroughs, past business districts and ethnic enclaves, to the tenements of the Lower East Side (LEFT).

An electric train of the Third Avenue El en route to Wall Street (RIGHT). The earlier steam engines were constantly starting fires in the awnings and curtains of the older buildings they brushed past, putting the city's emblematic fire escapes to good use.

moving walkways, even pneumatic tubes shooting passenger capsules the length of the city. The first line to be built, in 1867, used cable car technology, but soon the El settled on routine steam locomotives.

By 1893 Els were carrying half a million passengers a day, with routes starting at the southern tip of Manhattan and delivering farmworkers to the tomato fields of the Bronx. Across the East River, residents of downtown Brooklyn could take an El to the seashore at Coney Island. By 1903, all Manhattan's lines had been electrified.

What goes up in 1887 (ABOVE)
comes down in the 1940s (RIGHT).
As they built the 30-ft.-high tracks,
the Manhattan Elevated Railroad
Company compensated property
owners for loss of light; a payback was
expected when that amenity returned.
The early steam trains were often
scheduled at two-minute intervals,
and traveled at 15mph. By 1921,
the electrified system was carrying a
million passengers a day.

SIDEWALK VAULTS
NOT DISTURBED

SUB VAULT

EDISON

GAS GAS

WATER

SEWER

3 FT.

LOCAL TRAINS

EXPRESS TRAINS

26 FT.

PRESENT FOUNDATION OF
MODERN BUILDINGS

THE SUBWAY

Underground to the boroughs

FIRST CONTRACT
Rapid Transit Subway
Construction Company

COMPLETED
1900

How to cut and cover (LEFT).
*A 1905 magazine illustration
shows how the subway builders
will neatly install four tracks
under Broadway without
disturbing foundations, sidewalk
vaults, or pipe galleries. When
demand for service came from
parts of the city not connected
by avenues, the reality of
subway tunneling* (BELOW)
became messier.

AFTER THE FIVE BOROUGHS came together as Greater New York in 1898, the subway was to be crucial to the bonding process. These were not naturally compatible communities. Brooklyn, already a proud and bustling city in its own right, was wary of being subsumed by its flashy island neighbor. Did the market gardeners of Queens belong in a concrete conurbation? Citizens of the Bronx, though living a more rustic lifestyle than the community south of the Harlem River, were more enthusiastic, figuring that the high values of Manhattan real estate might spread northward. Staten Island, where a small farm could be bought for a down payment of $10, was the sleepiest of the boroughs, and living down a reputation as a haunt of malaria.

In fact, the subway never got to Staten Island, which was to remain, and revel in, being a patch of "small-town America." But the subway eased the pressure on congested Manhattan, allowing its high earners to commute from suburbs, thus spending money and so encouraging service industries off the

island. Lines were boldly built out to vacant, rural tracts, sparking the development of Astoria, Flushing, Flatbush. In the 1920s, refugees from the overcrowded tenements left for a better life in the Bronx as apartment blocks were built around the new Pelham Bay terminal.

Paris and London had routed their first urban railroad systems underground; New York, coming later to the idea, planned two fundamental differences from those pioneer services. Each route would have four tracks rather than two so that express trains would not be impeded by locals stopping at every station.

And there would be one fare – a nickel – whatever the length of the journey. (A century later, disgruntled Londoners calculated that traveling a mile on their Underground cost more than a supersonic mile on Concorde.) The promise was, Manhattan to Coney Island,

Earlier commuters traveled by ferry, horse-drawn streetcar, or the exposed El; now the subway offered protection from the winter winds (ABOVE). By World War I, it was carrying a billion passengers a year (RIGHT).

5 cents; Times Square to Flushing, 5 cents …. Families could decide where to live without worrying about travel costs. Not until 1948 did the fare increase.

Tunneling any great distance through the city's rock underpinnings was too technically challenging for the times, so construction began as "cut and cover" – dig a ditch, lay the track, and put the street back on top. In October 1904, Mayor McClellan drove the first train from the station near City Hall, through Bleecker Street Station and on to 103rd Street – "at breakneck speed," according to the motorman beside him. In four years, 8,000 men laid 20 miles of track, three-fourths of it underground. Tunnels under the rivers took tracks to Brooklyn and New Jersey. (Unconnected Staten Island got five new steel-hulled, state-of-the-art ferries as a consolation.) A complex private/public venture to enlarge the system, the Dual Contracts of 1913, had a cost of $300 million, the most expensive construction project at the time except for the Panama Canal.

With 250 miles of routes (and almost four times that amount of track) and more than 450 stations, this is the most extensive rapid transit system in the world.

Destination, New Jersey (LEFT).
Buses from the world's busiest bus
terminal, on Eighth Avenue at
42nd Street, ease down ramps to
join traffic entering the Lincoln
Tunnel, the world's busiest tunnel.
It was a twin-tubed facility when
this photograph was taken in
1951. A third tube, 8,000 ft.
long, was added in 1957.

A steam shovel clears the path
for the Holland Tunnel (RIGHT).
The first boring under the
Hudson, for railroad connections,
began in the 1870s but took
30 years to complete.

TUNNELS

Roads beneath the rivers

HOLLAND
ENGINEER
Clifford M. Holland

COMPLETED
1927

LINCOLN
BUILDERS
Port of New York Authority

COMPLETED
1937

QUEENS–MIDTOWN
DESIGNER
Ole Singstad

COMPLETED
1940

BROOKLYN–BATTERY
DESIGNER
Ole Singstad

COMPLETED
1950

THE RAILROAD AND SUBWAY COMPANIES had long been burrowing their way out of the island, but it was not until the 1920s that the problem of clearing exhaust pollution from long tunnels was solved, and vehicular traffic could be routed under the rivers that encircled Manhattan.

The breakthrough was made by an engineer named Clifford Holland; in 1927 the twin-tubed tunnel named for him opened to traffic. At almost 9,000 ft., from Canal Street to Jersey City, it was at the time the world's longest underwater tunnel. Holland's ventilation system used electric fans on each shore to force air under the roadways and into circulation through curbside vents. Separate exhaust fans sucked out the diluted gases through ceiling extractors. The air was changed every 90 seconds.

*Inside the Holland Tunnel are
cast iron and concrete bores,
lined with clean white tiles
90 ft. below the surface of the
Hudson River* (BELOW). *It was
the Holland Tunnel's builders
who first gave motorists air fit
to breathe in a confined space.
Quarter-mile markers remind
drivers of the 30mph speed
limit, which was further
enforced by guards patrolling the
catwalk. By the late 1930s*
(FAR RIGHT) *12 million cars
a year were using the Holland
Tunnel's two tubes, paying 50
cents for the privilege.*

The Lincoln Tunnel was next, opening to traffic from West 39th Street to Weehawken, New Jersey, in 1937. When a third tube was added to the complex 20 years later, scrap metal from the dismantled El railroad was recycled into the structure. Then in 1940 the Queens–Midtown Tunnel, two two-lane tubes 6,500 ft. long and 95 ft. below the surface of the East River, took city traffic to the Long Island City district of Queens; it was to become important as a route to the city's airports.

Work on the Brooklyn–Battery Tunnel stopped almost as soon as it began: World War II intervened. By the time it opened in 1950 it had cost $80 million and eight lives. Cast-iron lined and white-tiled, its two tubes are the longest underwater tunnels in the USA, at almost two miles. An octagonal tower, the tunnel's mid-point ventilator, is a landmark on Governor's Island.

The builders' platforms may look primitive (ABOVE) but well-learned lessons and new techniques allowed the Queens–Midtown Tunnel to be built in three years – half the time it took to complete the city's first vehicular tunnel. It opened to traffic in 1940. Work on the last and longest of the city's tunnels, the Brooklyn–Battery, began that year but was suspended during World War II. The Brooklyn entrance is seen (LEFT) taking the strain of a transit strike in 1966.

CENTRAL PARK

Green heart of Manhattan

ARCHITECT-IN-CHIEF
Frederick Law Olmsted, with
Calvert Vaux

COMPLETED
1859

CENTRAL PARK was far from central when it was planned and named – way north of the huddled masses who most needed pastoral refreshment. But the visionaries who drew the Manhattan grid plan came to realize that the growing city must have a breathing space. What might have been leisure areas on the

Skaters in Central Park, 1910. Lakes like this took the place of former swamps. The park was intended to be "classless," but the wealthier citizens dominated it early on, parading around the carriage drives and riding horses on the bridle paths.

waterfront were occupied by noisy, dirty docks and shipyards. New building was relentlessly lining the frontages of the city blocks, leaving only the occasional open space where Broadway's meanderings and the long-engraved pattern of downtown left unusable plots. And as yet another speculator-fueled stock market crash, in 1857, took its painful toll on the poorest of New Yorkers, making a park for their benefit was a public works project that might employ and calm a discontented citizenry.

The chosen site covered 843 acres – twice the size of Monaco – from Fifth Avenue in the east to Eighth Avenue in the west, from

Olmsted (ABOVE) was anxious that no trace of the city would sully views within the park. But even in 1860 (TOP), gray silhouettes appear on the horizon. He went on to further park commissions in the five boroughs.

When the park was first proposed, surveyors carried side-arms for fear of 5,000 squatters who rightly suspected their motives. A plan by Egbert Viele was accepted by Washington Irving, president of the Central Park advisory board, but, after much politicking, it was back to the drawing board for a design competition. Olmsted and Vaux's winning entry (RIGHT) ingeniously allowed for crosstown commercial traffic, but hid it from view; and, with bridges, underpasses, and overpasses, created separated networks for carriages, riders, and pedestrians.

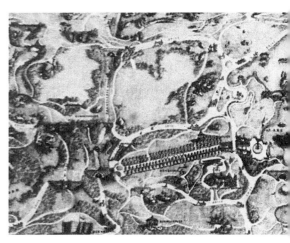

59th Street up to 106th Street, and later 110th Street, where marshes and rock outcrops made the land unappealing to the city's ravenous property developers. A design competition was won by a team of the English-born architect Calvert Vaux, and a landscape architect-farmer-writer named Frederick Olmsted. Once the shantytowns of Irish pig farmers and German gardeners were cleared and a whole black settlement to the north razed, they set to work on their "Greensward Plan."

Man would mould nature, bringing the countryside into the city, creating habitats for birds, rabbits, and squirrels, punctuating the vistas with rustic bridges and statuary. As many as 20,000 men worked on "19th century America's greatest work of art." They dug ditches so that crosstown commercial traffic stayed out of sight. They blasted out lakes for boaters and anglers and winter skaters. They planted nearly 300,000 trees and shrubs and laid carriage drives, pedestrian walkways, and bridle paths. Landscaping created the illusion that the park went on for ever.

The architects' social vision was to create a great democratic meeting ground where all classes, at leisure, could mingle. It was to be some time before that ambition was fulfilled. When the park opened in 1859, the streetcar fares might amount to a week's wages for a family from the tenements, and if they did make the journey the park police banned picnicking, playing ball, or walking on the grass.

So Central Park was at first a preserve of the merchant class and the wealthy, who ostentatiously paraded their carriages along the grand, tree-lined promenade of the Mall, skated on the ponds in winter, listened to summer afternoon concerts, and admired the token flock of sheep grazing in a meadow. Progressive reformers slowly eroded the rules and public and private benefactors provided playgrounds and ballfields, and developed the zoo, the park's most popular feature.

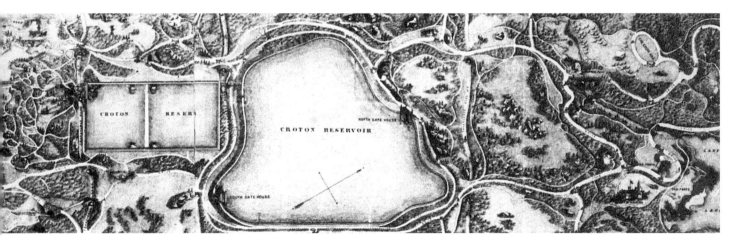

"The Mall is
an indispensable
provision in any great
park, and we know no
great park anywhere
in which there is a
finer promenade."

SCRIBNER'S MONTHLY

Open spaces for all

CREATING PUBLIC PARKS was not a priority in early American urban planning. The wealthy men directing the processes had easy access to the countryside. It took a while for them to realize that local open spaces were needed for those who could not summon a carriage and horses to escape the increasingly debilitating frenzy of metropolitan existence, its overcrowding, noise, and pollution.

In fact, cemeteries became the first "scanty patches of verdure" for city dwellers – Laurel Hill in Philadelphia, Graceland in Chicago, Green-Wood in Brooklyn – where families picnicked among the tombstones on summer Sundays. And the association with graveyards continued when inner city parks became more commonplace: Bryant Park, the smudge of green alongside the New York Public Library, is on the site of a "potter's field," a paupers' burial ground, as is Washington Square Park in Greenwich Village.

Another valuable land legacy for park builders was decommissioned military property. When Manhattan no longer felt the need for defensive batteries of artillery at its southern tip, Battery Park took their place. The park at Madison Square replaced an arsenal, barracks, and a potter's field. And indeed, the headquarters of the Parks Department is the Arsenal, a former ammunition store in Central Park.

Walt Whitman used his newspaper, *The Eagle*, to agitate for a park in Brooklyn, and was quickly rewarded with Fort Greene Park. Olmsted and Vaux, fresh from the success of their Central Park, went on to build Prospect Park in the borough;

Central Park's designers, Olmsted and Vaux, went on to landscape Prospect Park in Brooklyn, whose lawns, woods, and waters, it is often claimed, compose America's finest urban park. Commanding the main entrance is the Soldiers and Sailors' Memorial Arch of Grand Army Plaza (LEFT).

In 1831, a marsh was drained and an English square copied to create Gramercy Park (RIGHT) at Lexington Avenue and 21st Street. Only owners of the surrounding houses had the "golden keys" to the gates.

CITY HALL SQUARE ~ SUBW

Olmsted was pleased to notice "people coming together, and with an evident glee in the prospect." He also thought such places "divert men from unwholesome, vicious and destructive habits."

The Bronx, traditionally the greenest of the five boroughs, has two parks bigger than Central Park: Pelham Bay Park, edged by nine miles of Long Island Sound shoreline, and Van Cortlandt Park, named for a one-time mayor of New York whose family farmed the land until the city bought it in the 1880s.

In Queens, the journalist who brought guilty attention to the misery of the Lower East Side in *How the Other Half Lives* is remembered in the name of Jacob Riis Park. Flushing Meadows/Corona Park occupies the site cleared by Parks Commissioner Robert Moses to stage two New York World's Fairs.

It was Moses, of course, who turfed, planted, and watered oases for the modern city, landscaping lots under and around the highways and bridges he built, and notably completing the long-anticipated Riverside Park on a narrow strip along the Hudson River, north from 72nd Street. He also built more than 250 children's playgrounds in the city (but only two of them in black neighborhoods).

In the 1960s, the "vest pocket park" movement set about rehabilitating the small vacant lots that punctuate frontages of stone and steel. Mobilizing Operation Green Thumb, residents of the East Village converted dozens of unofficial waste dumps into communal gardens, warding off developers, parking lot operators, and politicians eager to encourage building that would enlarge the city's tax base.

Two hundred years after a grand plan that seemed to root out every tree and blade of grass, New York has the nation's largest acreage of urban parks.

City Hall Square busy with commuters in 1910 (LEFT). *Its subway station was the city's first. Once known as the Commons, this is where New Yorkers traditionally rioted, protested, and celebrated. The British hanged a governor for treason nearby; here, the Declaration of Independence was read publicly for the first time.*

Jacob Riis, whose images of Lower East Side squalor triggered the city's social conscience, took this 1899 photograph (ABOVE) *of ground being cleared to make way for Jefferson Park — the kind of project he advocated. It was, though, far north of his constituency: at 112th Street beside the East River.*

A history in effigies and arches

NEW YORK HAS THE MODERN world's most famous monument – the Statue of Liberty, which gives thanks and tribute to the city itself and all its citizens. But New York's story is short in comparison with those of the great European cities, not long enough to grow heroes and legends in any number and then immortalize them in bronze and marble, as in London, Paris, or Rome.

And there's reason for ambivalence about the virtue of some local heroes: extravagant contributors to the city's wellbeing often did so from fortunes based on ruthless exploitation of cotton-pickers, ironworkers, and Chinese railroad gangs. Much-loved, sequentially re-elected politicians, candidates for the sculptor's chisel, openly and recklessly raided the city's coffers.

With the city's *raison d'être* being the pursuit of wealth, its most notable monuments are those that spectacularly successful men built in their own names – the Woolworth Building, Rockefeller Center, Trump Tower. In the surrounding streets, strictly north, south, east, and west, there is little pause or space for hero worship. The idea is to "squeeze profit out of every inch of the dirt."

But there could be no doubt about honoring Ulysses S. Grant, commander of Union forces in the Civil War, 18th president of the United States, who briefly lived in New York

George Washington dominates Union Square: an 1856 equestrian statue by Henry Kirke Brown (LEFT). *It was commissioned by wealthy local businessmen anxious to show their loyalty to the Union as sympathy for secession stirred in the South.*

Flags and flowers bedeck a grand arch in Washington Square Park for the 1889 centenary of Washington's inauguration (RIGHT). *In fact, this was the wood and plaster prototype for a marble version the architect Stanford White would build on the site.*

Dewey Arch, over Fifth Avenue at 23rd Street (LEFT), *did not last. It was made of wood and plaster, a temporary commemoration of Admiral Dewey's victory over the Spanish in Manila Bay in 1898. Dewey led a triumphant parade through it in 1899, but when his presidential ambitions were thwarted by Theodore Roosevelt, the public appeal to raise funds for a permanent memorial failed. A year later, the arch was in the city dump.*

Grant's Tomb (RIGHT), *overlooking the Hudson at Morningside Heights, is the largest mausoleum in the country. Behind the Doric columns, the interior copies the Paris tomb of Napoleon Bonaparte. Grant's widow, Julia, is also interred here.*

and is the only president to be buried there. After its opening in 1897, Grant's Tomb quickly became the city's most popular tourist attraction as streams of carriages made the pilgrimage up Riverside Drive.

Other statesmen have their likenesses displayed in bronze and stone; Washington on horseback in Washington Square and Lincoln nearby, and again in a Brooklyn garden.

Staten Island honors an Italian patriot: Giuseppe Garibaldi, who added Sicily and Naples to the kingdom of Italy, as it was then, lived there briefly and worked as a candlemaker. His cottage at Stapleton was preserved under a classically columned stone shelter.

ZOOS

Animal kingdoms

FIRST THERE WERE MENAGERIES, now there are wildlife conservation centers. Since the showman P.T. Barnum paraded a particularly large elephant through the streets of Manhattan in 1882, attitudes to displaying wild animals have been continually changing. So too have the structures to house them, becoming ever more naturalistic.

Central Park's designers had no taste for caging animals. But just as tourists cannot resist throwing coins into any available fountain, citizens who were determined to have fauna among the park's flora plied the staff with gifts of mice and deer. The menagerie to house them, set up at the Arsenal, grew into a full-scale zoo. By the 1930s it was in disgraceful disrepair. Parks Commissioner Robert Moses rebuilt it, then it was heavily renovated again in the 1980s. The Children's Zoo, meanwhile, had become a major attraction, featuring a redwood Noah's Ark as its centerpiece.

Moses also rebuilt Brooklyn's Prospect Park Zoo during the Depression. Bringing it up to modern standards in the early 1990s required a four-year closure and $36 million. And Moses had a hand in the Queens Zoo, allocating space for it as he signed over the Flushing Meadows site of the World's Fairs to the city. This center, too, had a major updating, in 1992. The Staten Island Zoo opened in 1936, specializing in snakes and other reptiles whose quarters have also become more user-friendly over the years.

But it is the Bronx Zoo that is New York's world-class facility, and its development and renewal have been continuous processes since it opened in 1899. A vast, domed elephant house was built in 1908. The breakthrough in banishing iron-barred cages came in 1941 when moats encircled and secured the "savannah" of the

Central Park Zoo, the city's first, spread out around the Arsenal (LEFT), the arms store that became a makeshift menagerie. The building has served several city purposes – police precinct, weather bureau, home of the American Museum of Natural History. It is now headquarters of the Parks Department.

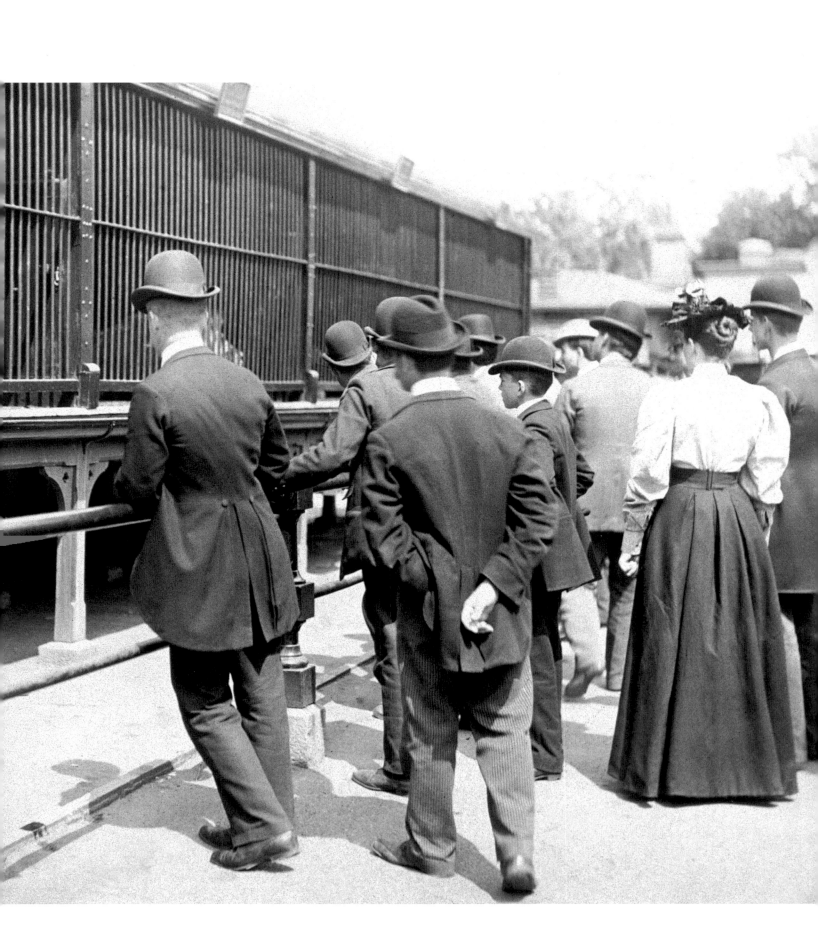

African Plains exhibit. The World of Darkness (1961) manipulates artificial lighting to reverse the waking cycles of nocturnal animals so that they are active for daytime visitors. Then came the Lila Acheson Wallace World of Birds (Mrs. Wallace was the co-founder of *The Reader's Digest*), a cluster of concrete cylinders, without wing-damaging corners, where zoo-goers observe high-flying species from ramps at treetop height.

The Bronx Zoo is the nation's largest city zoo. Amid its dramatic complexes, the Wildlife Conservation Society, formerly the New York Zoological Society, administers internationally important programs in environmental education and species preservation.

CEMETERIES

The city's last resting places

BURYING THE DEAD poses a problem for growing cities. No sooner has a green field site been consecrated for the purpose than its sanctity is threatened by the needs of the living: for housing, workplaces, and infrastructure. Successive maps of neatly circular Paris, for instance, show how graveyards placed well outside the city limits were subsumed at regular intervals; most dramatically, the one on the once-remote hill of Montmartre.

In early 19th-century New York, paupers were interred at Washington Square; in 1823 their remains were removed to the distant quietude of Fifth Avenue and 40th Street, later to Fourth Avenue and 50th Street, and finally off Manhattan altogether, to Ward's Island.

Burials within the city were banned in 1847, and the towns and villages of Queens to the east of Long Island City soon had so many cemeteries that the area became known as "the city of the dead." Poor Irish were buried at Old Calvary; generations of the Lawrence family, including a mayor of New York, lie in Lawrence's Cemetery in Bayside.

Green-Wood Cemetery in Brooklyn was a favored last resting place. It had been landscaped by Major David B. Douglass around the city's highest elevation, a modest 216 ft. With four lakes and miles of wooded walks, it became a popular, if accidental, park – and, indeed, the inspiration for Central Park. Quakers were interred in the still-immaculate Friends' Cemetery in Prospect Park. Brooklyn also has a National Cemetery at Cypress Hills, now closed to new interments.

Woodlawn, between Webster and Jerome Avenues in the Bronx, opened in 1863, and 300,000 graves have been dug there since. It was, and remains, the city's most elegant cemetery, home to Woolworth, Huntington, and Whitney family mausoleums.

The Vanderbilt family is buried beside the Moravian Cemetery on Staten Island, in a mausoleum designed by Richard Morris Hunt, architect of their mansions, on a plot landscaped by Olmsted. Unidentified poor are now buried in unmarked graves on Hart Island, laid to rest by inmates of the Rikers Island prison.

The Roman Catholic Calvary Cemetery in Queens (RIGHT) has 3 million graves, the most in the United States. Parcels of land have been added since it opened in 1848 as a burial ground for poor Lower East Siders.

A drummer accompanies mourners leaving Green-Wood Cemetery in 1899 (BELOW). The flamboyantly Gothic gatehouse, flanked by pavilions with multicolored roofs, was designed by Richard Upjohn.

Elaborate headstones sit among the trees of Green-Wood Cemetery (BELOW LEFT). The reburial here of De Witt Clinton, mayor and state governor, made cemetery burials acceptable; previously, notable figures had been interred in family plots or churchyards.

BOTANICAL GARDENS

Combining science with pleasure

THE TITLE ROLE IN *A Tree Grows in Brooklyn* is played by the ailanthus, the city's emblematic tree, a tough deciduate whose seedlings take hold in any urban crevice, growing to punctuate the sidewalks with sprouts of foliage that ignore acidic rain and polluted air.

An Asian native, the ailanthus made its American landfall at the Bronx home of the New York Botanical Garden, brought there by Samuel Parsons, Jr., one of the Garden's founding figures and a pioneer horticulturist. It acclimatized among the hemlock, truly a New York native, in a 40-acre arboretum astride the Bronx River.

The Garden – 240 acres in all, opened in 1891 – aspired to be the country's counterpart to the Royal Botanical Gardens at Kew, in England, and modeled its iron and glass Victorian greenhouses on those at Kew. The site had been the property of the Lorillard tobacco family; the snuff mill that turned their produce into powder remains a feature of the Garden.

Like the zoos that are, in New York, their close neighbors, botanical gardens exist to promote the exotic. The architecture reflects the artifice. The Brooklyn garden, given an early and enriching boost by waste from the breweries and stables that preceded it in Prospect Park, features a Shinto shrine in its Japanese landscape garden. Staten Island has a Chinese Scholars' Garden that copies a Ming Dynasty contemplative retreat.

New Yorkers know it's spring when the trees blossom in the Brooklyn Botanic Garden (ABOVE AND RIGHT). The Garden first opened to the public in 1910, a time when such facilities were generally restricted to botanists and plantsmen.

PUBLIC BUILDINGS

The services and machinery of state

MOST CITIES WITH IMAGES AS powerful as New York's are their nations' capitals, required to build compounds for bureaucrats alongside forums suiting the self-esteem of the people's representatives. New York only had to take care of itself, and started out modestly: the original administrative headquarters was a tavern.

A first Federal Hall, so-named in 1699 when New York had a commanding role in the colony's affairs, acted as a more sober city center. That was demolished after 1812, when municipal business was transferred to the elegant new City Hall, a Classical design topped by a cupola that offered views across a pastoral countryside.

Now there was need for courthouses and prisons, public libraries, and a post office. As the city limits pushed north, there were visions for a civic center in new territory, where the infrastructure of governance might be spaciously housed in edifices as grandiose as those the bankers and bishops were building. But the politicians were against distancing themselves from the Wall Street money machine. Construction sites encroached on the oasis of City Hall Park. Grand plans smothered small sites. The city that had the vision to stake out Central Park would later regret missing the opportunity to dedicate another district to municipal, state, and federal business.

In such an introspective environment, malfeasance was hard to hide. In 1871, the *New York Times* noticed that Mayor Tweed's cronies had somehow "spent" $12 million on building the New York County Courthouse, against a budget of $800,000. London's contemporaneous Houses of Parliament cost less. A carpenter was paid $350,000 for a month's work; tables and chairs for a meeting room cost $180,000. Mayor Tweed died in jail. The corruption of the Tammany Hall political machine was exposed for all to see.

The Tombs detention center (RIGHT), *named for the Egyptian-tomb inspiration of its predecessor, and its dismal appearance, was one of the institutional buildings taking prime space in the financial district. The Bridge of Sighs* (BELOW) *connected it to the Criminal Courts Building. New facilities were built on the same site in 1983.*
WITHERS & DICK, 1897

The French architect Joseph F. Mangin won the competition to design City Hall (BELOW LEFT). *His Scottish partner, John McComb, who supervised the work, did not quite fulfill their ambitions: after budget overruns, the city stipulated a cheaper, brownstone back for the building – a side "nobody will ever see."*

The United States Courthouse and Post Office (TOP) took a large chunk out of City Hall Park, to the dismay of the overcrowded neighborhood. Dressed as a French town hall, it was in fact a fortress, with 10-ft.-thick, iron-reinforced walls, and armor-plated window frames. City Hall Park regained the site in the 1930s.
ALFRED B. MULLETT, 1875

The New York General Post Office (ABOVE), as grand and Classical as its ill-fated neighbor, Pennsylvania Station, was designed by the same architects. Built on steel and concrete stilts above the railroad yard, it had a pneumatic tube mail service to the Brooklyn General Post Office.
McKIM, MEAD & WHITE, 1913

The second Federal Hall, now known as the Federal Hall National Memorial (RIGHT) served as a U.S. Custom House. It is one of the city's great historical landmarks and is just in sight of another, Trinity Church, at the left of the photograph. The statue of George Washington commemorates the fact that he took the oath of office on this site.
TOWN & DAVIS, 1842

Bequeathed private collections prompted the founding of the New York Public Library, now one of the city's proudest institutions, and one of the world's finest libraries. On the site of the old Croton Reservoir at Fifth Avenue and 42nd Street, its white Vermont marble has weathered since the 1911 photograph (TOP RIGHT). Couchant lions, stone nymphs, and fountains make the long forecourt a favorite resting place (LEFT). More than 600 chairs at oak tables served students in the Main Reading Room, seen in the 1920s (BELOW RIGHT). There are branches of the library throughout the city. CARRERE & HASTINGS, 1911

The trading places of Wall Street

EVERY OTHER KIND OF commercial activity has been tempted uptown, even out of town altogether, but the business of money has stayed resolutely rooted in its first base, Wall Street. Financial trading began there when the bonds issued to pay for the Revolutionary War became negotiable securities. Legend has it that 24 brokers sat under a tree on a spring day in 1792 to draw up the "Buttonwood Agreement," ground rules for trading, and that the New York Stock Exchange arose nearby, at Wall Street and Broad Street.

The continuing loyalty to the locality has been ascribed to David Rockefeller, who demonstrated support for Lower Manhattan by building new headquarters for his Chase Manhattan Bank at Chase Manhattan Plaza, between Pine and Liberty Streets, in 1960.

Other towers of steel and glass have arisen around Wall Street, many with nameplates harking back to the early days of New York wealth. The recent tower of the Morgan Bank is a reminder of John Pierpont Morgan, the most powerful of all 19th-century bankers. Morgan financed Thomas Edison's power station on Pearl Street and his own office was the first in the city to be electrically lit.

The nearby Morgan Guaranty Trust Building still bears the scars of a 1920 attack, supposedly by Bolsheviks. And other fragments have been respected by later builders: marble cornerstones and granite columns, first dragged from the river landings by teams of oxen, are preserved in walls made of more modern compounds.

Standing over a fortune – five underground floors of the world's gold reserves – the Federal Reserve Bank (LEFT) occupies an entire block along Liberty Street, three blocks north of Wall Street. Its design inspiration was the fortified palaces of Renaissance Florence.
YORK & SAWYER, 1924

Above the Corinthian columns of the neo-Classical New York Stock Exchange (ABOVE RIGHT), the pediment sculpture depicts "Integrity Protecting the Works of Man." Inside (RIGHT), "horseshoe" trading posts ready for business in 1904.
GEORGE B. POST, 1903

UNIVERSITIES
Seats of learning

The Low Memorial Library (TOP) *set the tone for construction on the Columbia campus. Seth Low was president of the college at the time of its move.*

*Bronx Community College took over the University Heights campus of New York University, including the Gothic Shepard Hall (*SECOND FROM TOP*) and the Hall of Fame for Great Americans (*ABOVE*). There are niches, not all filled, for 150 notables in the semi-circular granite colonnade of the Hall of Fame (*OPPOSITE*). Twenty-nine busts were in place for the 1901 dedication.*

*Released from its inner city constrictions, Columbia had found space for a football field by 1915 (*RIGHT*).*

NEW YORK DID NOT AT first aspire to be a center of learning; the more morally motivated communities of Boston and Philadelphia were better suited to that sort of profitless activity. Nevertheless, in the 1750s, eight students gathered in Trinity Church schoolhouse, as the first enrollment of King's College. By 1760, the college had a purpose-built home to the west of Broadway, overlooking the Hudson River. Its cupola was topped by a crown. That, and the name, disappeared after Independence.

Columbia grew quickly, in size and prestige. But noise and overcrowding soon overwhelmed its neighborhood, and the everyday vice on the streets distracted students. Over the years, the university spread around a midtown site, erecting much-admired buildings by the architect C. C. Haight, himself a Columbia graduate. His inspiration was "English Collegiate," the Gothic styles of Oxford and Cambridge.

But always working against the concept of a contained campus was the grid plan that the city was reluctant to interrupt. And, it was considered, the right atmosphere for fraternity and diligent learning could not be achieved if the students, mostly from city families, went home at night.

The distant rocky ridge of Morningside Heights, west of Harlem, was the answer. There was already the basis of a campus in place, the Bloomingdale Insane Asylum, a social blight being pressured out by prosperous new residents of the area; and a cathedral was being built nearby, a suitable neighbor. In 1897, Columbia concentrated on this location, where an ordered academic community could grow.

The architects McKim, Mead & White, builders of mansions and monuments, set out the grand plans, as they did for New York University at University Heights – NYU Uptown. The women of Barnard College were housed in a style that matched the Columbia campus, on the other side of Broadway.

Daniel Chester French's statue, Alma Mater, welcomed students to the Low Library. In fact, despite its refined, classical form, this was not a successful library building, and became instead the university's administrative headquarters.

EARLY SKYSCRAPERS

Exploring the new dimension

WITH FRONTAGES on the rigid grid avenues and cross streets filling at the rate of 10 miles a year, Manhattan would soon be full, its residential and commercial populations confined to mostly four- and five-story buildings. To go much higher, given the technology of the time, would have required buildings in the style of Egypt's Pyramids, with every layer of masonry bearing the weight of the entire load above it.

But there was news from Chicago: architects were bolting together columns and crossbeams of wrought iron, soon to be steel, to take the strain in taller buildings. The infilling walls and windows weighed only on the particular girder that supported them. Walls could be as thin at the base of a building as at the top; if it suited them, bricklayers could as readily work from the top floor down as from the bottom up. Furthermore, an engineer named Elisha Graves Otis had devised a safety device for an elevator so that it would not crash to the bottom of its shaft if the pulley rope broke. The daunting prospect of climbing stairs no longer put a limit on the number of floors.

The rise and rise of New York could begin. The E.V. Haughwout & Co. Store of 1857, an early department store on Broadway at Broome Street, hinted at what was to come: an external skeleton of curved and decorated iron, infilled with windows, and an Otis elevator to carry customers to light and airy retail displays. In 1888, Bradford Gilbert's Tower Building had reached 13 stories. By 1929 New York had more than 180 buildings more than 20 stories high — half the nation's skyscraper total — including the 1913 60-story Woolworth Building, which remained the tallest in the world for a full 15 years.

New York's schist bedrock provided perfect underpinning for skyscrapers: there was no fear of them settling excessively under their own weight. Given their start in Chicago, "the windy city," skyscraper architects and structural engineers paid early attention to the most powerful force affecting tall buildings — the wind. They were to arrive at a specification: "wind drift," the movement at the top of the building, should not exceed the height of the building divided by 500. Thus, the 1,368 ft.-high World Trade Center had a wind drift of just 3 ft. at the top.

Early low-rise skyscrapers had semi-rigid bolted joints, allowing a degree of flexibility. Later, the central

core, a continuous concrete shaft containing elevators and staircases, acted as the wind brace. By the time the World Trade Center was built, computer-aided engineering calculations had led to light, strong, full-height tubes of complex steel lattices capable of withstanding storms and earthquakes, though not suicidal airborne attacks. The projections are that refinements of this engineering will support structures 150 stories high.

With the construction difficulties being overcome as they arose, the environmental and social dynamics of skyscrapers had to be addressed. The cliché, "the canyons of Wall Street," came about from the unrestrained rise of monoliths. In 1916 the city imposed some rules. There should be setbacks in new buildings at human-scale heights – five stories up in the case of the Empire State Building. The setback specification would relate to the width of the adjoining streets – usually one and a half times. Then further graduated setbacks were required until the tower was allowed to rise unhindered, but on no more than 25 percent of the area of the plot. The zoning authorities later devised an arcane way of measuring buildings' shadows: the calculation would be made at 3PM on December 21, the winter solstice. Thus the Empire State Building's official shadow is more than a mile long.

Before high-rise building, the lower the room, be it apartment, hotel, or office, the greater the convenience, and the higher the rent. That changed when the elevator could whisk tenants to a view of the sky and the city below. Skyscraper developers quickly realized that the more extravagant the view, the more they could earn, and they took to buying and leasing depressed and decaying brownstones on neighboring plots to prevent development that might overshadow their properties.

An early statement in the corporate skyscraper race. The stepped pyramid that topped its headquarters on Wall Street became the Bankers Trust Company's symbol. The previous tall building on the site lasted just 13 years.
TROWBRIDGE & LIVINGSTON, 1912

TIMES TOWER

Symbol of a free press

ARCHITECT
Cyrus L.W. Eidlitz

COMPLETED
1904

RENOVATION
Smith, Smith, Haines,
Lundberg & Waehler

COMPLETED
1965

NUMBER ONE TIMES SQUARE was at the symbolic heart of the city. It's where the presses thundered with "all the news that's fit to print," repeating the headlines in a girdle of flashing white lights around the building; it's where New Yorkers gathered, and gather still, for the luminous ball to drop at the stroke of the New Year.

Yet the building never achieved the iconic status of the other wedge-shaped tower that was built at around the same time, the Flatiron Building. Perhaps the vulgarity of the surroundings, the sleaze of Times Square, distracted New Yorkers from this powerful presence pointing north, where Broadway and Seventh Avenue intersect at 42nd Street.

Twenty-six stories high, Times Tower was faced in white glazed terracotta, the austerity relieved by confident Gothic and Renaissance details. The *New York Times* soon moved out, but retained ownership. By the 1960s, when the Allied Chemical Corporation bought it, new zoning laws prevented an equally big, new building from arising on the site. So the tower was stripped to its frame and its facings replaced.

The skeleton of box columns and girder beams reaches the 17th floor (LEFT). The old Metropolitan Opera House is three blocks behind, to the south. The skeleton is revealed again, 60 years later (RIGHT). It was then reclad in concrete panels faced with an inch of Vermont marble. This clean, bland face seemed oddly out of place in brash Times Square and was soon overlaid with neon and billboards (which are said to earn more rent than the office space behind them). A 1970s proposal to strip the building once more and resurface it in reflective glass failed to materialize.

FLATIRON BUILDING

A triangular triumph

ARCHITECT
Daniel H. Burnham & Co.

COMPLETED
1902

STILL SPECTACULAR AFTER ALL THESE YEARS, the Flatiron Building of 1902 won immediate respect as an imaginative expression of the city's faith in skyscrapers. It was designed by Daniel H. Burnham, one of the great Chicago skyscraper pioneers, to make dramatic use of a triangular site where Broadway carved across the city's grid plan at 23rd Street.

Behind the 6 ft.-wide prow, which seems to be bearing down on Madison Square Park, the building contained many forward-thinking ideas about the housekeeping of skyscrapers. It had a built-in fire control system, and an electrical generator to make it self-sufficient for energy needs.

In its early days, the Flatiron Building, properly named the Fuller Building, was best known for its least important attribute: the downdraft phenomenon that plagued the canyons between early skyscrapers was first noticed here. Voyeurs gathered for a glimpse of ankle as swirling winds lifted the petticoats of the elegant shoppers on Ladies' Mile.

The steel skeleton is clad in limestone facing blocks to bring a sturdy demeanor to the slim tower (LEFT). The Flatiron, 300 ft. high, was one of the first tall structures not needing to be walled from the bottom up; the frame took the strain. A heavy, richly decorated cornice in Italian Rennaissance style would complete the most photogenic and most photographed building of its day (ABOVE).

"The
Woolworth
Building will be
New York's true
fame. It does not
scrape the sky.
It greets it."

THE REV. S. PARKES CADMAN,
at the opening ceremony

WOOLWORTH BUILDING

A tower of nickels and dimes

ARCHITECT
Cass Gilbert

COMPLETED
1913

THE WORLD'S TALLEST HABITABLE BUILDING OF ITS DAY – at 792 ft., almost three times as high as the instantly famous Flatiron Building – could not depend on the bedrock anchorage that underpins so many New York high-rises. Architect Cass Gilbert sank caissons 100 ft. down into an unstable mix of mud and water, filled them with concrete, and then began what would be acclaimed as the Cathedral of Commerce, or, as Gilbert himself more earthily put it, "a machine for making money out of the land." Twenty-nine elevators carried 14,000 tenants to their work stations, demonstrating the potential for high-density accommodation on a restricted site.

On its Broadway frontage, the tower of Woolworth Building climbs to its full height without a setback, a hugely confident expression of what could be achieved with the new lightweight steel framing. The awe-inspiring height was emphasized by soaring vertical lines of white terracotta. Yet, among all this modernity, Gilbert looked back as far as the 12th century for his decorative effects. All the conceits of Gothic styling were there – in tourelles and finials, flying buttresses and gargoyles.

F. W. Woolworth, rich from his 1,000 five-and-ten cent stores, paid for the building in cash – $13.5 million.

Vaulted arches frame the sumptuous lobby. It is lined with extravagantly veined marble and glows with intricate detailing. Elevator doors and canopies are of wrought iron embossed with lacelike patterns.

The graceful design, with all its details emphasizing height, depended on the strength of a steel frame, here taking shape in 1911.

As the Bank of the Manhattan Company reached for the sky, workers could see the rival Chrysler Building rising four miles uptown. If the rivet catcher (LEFT) misses, a red-hot metal slug falls to the street.

BANK OF THE MANHATTAN COMPANY

Wall Street's high-flying loser

ARCHITECT
H. Craig Severance

COMPLETED
1929

THE LATE 1920S was a time when the city's prosperity seemed to have no limits. The stock market was soaring, almost doubling in value in one 12-month period. The truth was that it was losing touch with the underlying economy, as the Depression just over the horizon would show. But meanwhile the city's real estate developers were out to raise the skyline in step with the market. On one day in early 1929 they borrowed more than $70 million.

The race to be tallest truly became a spectator sport on the streets, and a matter of obsessive competitiveness for the professionals. One head-to-head contest symbolized the era: the Bank of the Manhattan Company versus the Chrysler Building.

The architects, H. Craig Severance and William Van Alen, had been colleagues and partners; now they became bitter rivals.

As each learned the other's secrets, it was back to the drawing board, again and again. Floors were added, penthouses, light beacons. When Severance topped the pyramidal tower of the Manhattan building with a 50-ft. flagpole to reach 927 ft., it seemed that victory was assured at 40 Wall Street. But the celebration was brief. A steel spire emerged through the top of the Chrysler Building: 1,046 ft.

The bank business was eventually merged into the Chase Manhattan; the building became the Trump Building.

The iron frames of earlier buildings were bolted together, but the steel girders and columns of the Bank of the Manhattan Company were joined with rivets, the work of riveting gangs, close-knit groups of four men who had to trust each other at perilous heights. Their bonding was such that if one

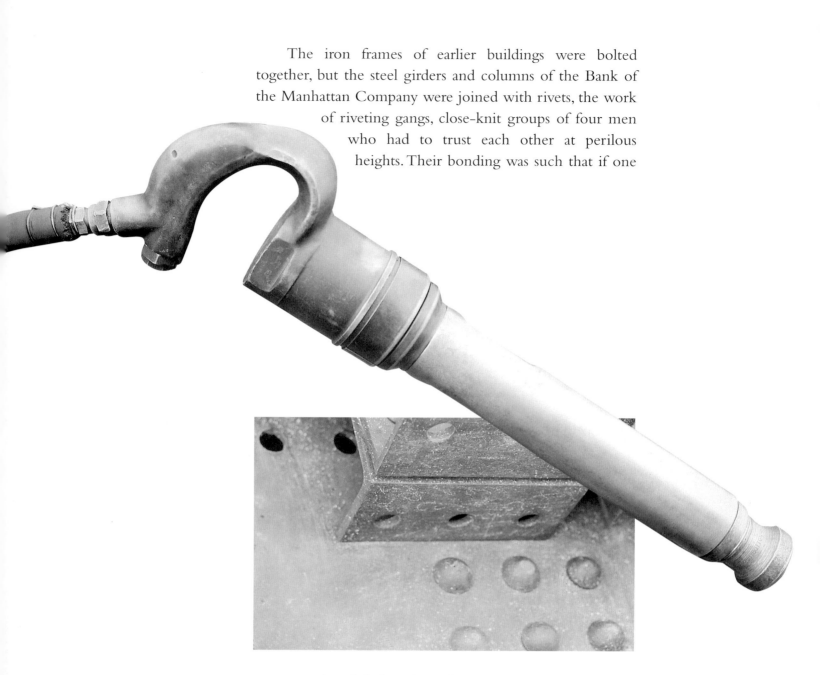

team member failed to show for work, the gang would be laid-off for the day.

The heater operated a coke forge. When the rivets were red-hot, he tossed them, one at a time, into the tin can held by the catcher, who might be 50 ft. away, usually on a floor above the heater so that the rivet reached him in a slow arc. Using long tongs, the catcher fished out the rivet, tapped it on a beam to disperse cinders, and rammed it into the aligned holes of the connecting steel plates. There it would be steadied by the bucker-up while the gunman drove it home with a "cricket," a compressed air gun.

The noise made by the cricket was deafening, the dangers of the process exaggerated in high winds, by the slippery surfaces on rainy days, and in the hand-numbing cold of winter. A day's pay was around $15, for eight hours, with a half-hour lunch break, and an expected work rate of about a rivet a minute.

GROWING TALLER: EARLY HIGH RISERS

MADISON SQUARE, ONCE A GLAMOROUS NEIGHBORHOOD, WAS
AN EARLY LOCATION FOR COMMERCIAL BUILDING, HERE BY
THE METROPOLITAN LIFE INSURANCE COMPANY.
Napoleon LeBrun, 1892

THE AMERICAN RADIATOR BUILDING FEATURED BLACK BRICK
AND GOLD PLATING – A DAYLIGHT COLOR EFFECT THAT WAS
REVERSED UNDER NIGHT-TIME ILLUMINATION.
Hood & Fouilhoux, 1924

A CAST-IRON FRAME INFILLED WITH WINDOWS AND AN OTIS
ELEVATOR MADE THE E.V. HAUGHWOUT & CO. STORE IDEAL
FOR ITS PURPOSE – RETAILING.
John P. Gaynor, 1857

THE UNION TRUST COMPANY BUILDING, AN ADMIRED, REFINED
APPROACH TO BUILDING TALLER, FACED TRINITY CHURCH
ACROSS ITS GRAVEYARD.
George B. Post, 1890

THE PUBLISHER JOSEPH B. PULITZER ADDED THE THE DOME
AND THREE-STORY PORTAL TO THE DESIGN OF HIS NEW YORK
WORLD BUILDING.
George B. Post, 1890

BRIEFLY THE WORLD'S TALLEST STRUCTURE, AT 612 FT.,
THE SINGER BUILDING HAD THE FIRST SKYSCRAPER
SPIRE. IT WAS RAZED IN 1968.
Ernest Flagg, 1908

THE MCGRAW HILL BUILDING WAS NOTABLE FOR ITS USE
OF COLOR – BANDS OF BLUE-GREEN TERRACOTTA TILES
SEPARATING ITS 33 FLOORS.
Raymond Hood, Grodley & Fouilhoux, 1930

THE CHRYSLER AND EMPIRE STATE BUILDINGS

A city's spectacular symbols

THE CHRSYLER
BUILDING
ARCHITECT
William Van Alen
COMPLETED
1930

THE EMPIRE STATE
BUILDING
ARCHITECT
Shreve, Lamb & Harmon
COMPLETED
1931

Watchers from one of the triangular windows of the Chrysler spire see the Empire State Building climbing skyward at the rate of a floor a day. The Chrysler's "spokes" were intended to echo the form of a car wheel.

TWO OF AMERICA'S AUTOMOBILE TYCOONS created the buildings that came to symbolize the sky-high ambitions of New York. Walter P. Chrysler, flamboyant and innovative – his Airflow sedan was America's first streamlined, aerodynamic car – decided to show his distaste for Detroit by building his headquarters in New York. John J. Raskob had created General Motors before founding the Empire State Corporation.

Finished first, in 1928, the singular Chrysler Building, an Art Deco emblem of modernism and progress, arose as a sleek rocket of white and gray bricks, decorated with gargoyles and hubcap motifs, and topped off in chrome steel. "An oversize jukebox," some called it; to others it is still the world's most beautiful skyscraper.

Chrysler's "advertising beacon" – the chrome steel spire was constructed inside the building and hoisted at the last moment to upstage the competition to be "New York's tallest."

Raskob had told his architect, "build a structure as tall as you can that won't fall over." Undaunted by the Depression – at least it made for an eager workforce – the builders demolished the Waldorf-Astoria Hotel and constructed a five-story base out to the property lines on Fifth Avenue and 33rd and 34th Streets, and then, above a series of setback recesses and indentations, the building climbed and climbed and climbed. In daily deliveries through the crowded city streets came 60,000 tons of Pittsburgh steel, 10 million bricks, 200,000 tons of limestone and granite. The frame went up at the rate of a story a day. In a year and 45 days the battle to dominate the New York skyline was won. The Empire State Building would be the world's tallest for 40 years.

Transatlantic airships were to moor at the mast on top of the Empire State Building, with passengers disembarking down a gangplank. Wind-thwarted blimp attempts killed the idea.

To photograph the final riveting at the Empire State Building, Lewis Hine was hung out on a rope almost a quarter of a mile above the city streets.

TWO NOTABLE PHOTOGRAPHERS have their names forever linked with these emblematic buildings. Raskob had Lewis W. Hine to record the Empire State's progress – a surprising choice given that Hine's reputation was based on documenting the saddest sides of New York life; the overcrowded tenements, child labor, poverty, and exploitation. He was "a reformer with a camera," hardly the qualification for creating a real estate prospectus. And indeed, Hine concentrated on the workers at the Empire State Building. His images of men nonchalantly walking along girders hundreds of feet above Fifth Avenue, swinging from cables and derricks, welding and riveting far above a cityscape backdrop, were to become a world-famous portfolio.

Margaret Bourke-White and the gargoyle that enchanted her. It was modeled on the radiator mascot of one of the Chrysler Corporation's current models.

For Margaret Bourke-White, the Chrysler Building was an irresistible subject. Already addicted to Art Deco, she was an elegant stylist, a pioneer of photo-journalism, whose first professional portfolio had been the buildings of Cleveland. She, too, became entranced with the sure-footedness and industry of the workforce; but even more by the stainless steel gargoyles that she watched being positioned outside the 61st floor. She persuaded Chrysler to lease her a room behind one of them, where she fitted out a studio with blond wood, aluminum, a glass desk, and a fish tank – furnishings as boldly Art Deco as the building around them. Bourke-White went on to become one of the most respected combat photographers of World War II and the Korean War.

No hard hats, no harnesses for the construction crews – but there was a safety line for the photographer, Lewis Hine. The standards of fearlessness for heights required of these workers had first been set by Native Americans of the Mohawk tribe. From their homelands near Montreal, they had been recruited to build bridges for the Canadian Pacific Railroad. Brought to New York, they were eagerly joined and emulated by recruits from the city's vast pool of unemployed men. Hine quickly lost his own fear of heights and delighted in close-up observation of derrickmen and welders, cement masons and bricklayers, and the four-man riveting teams working on the Empire State Building. The "connector" being hoisted to work (RIGHT) ignores the Chrysler Building behind him – the one they had to beat in the battle to be tallest.

ROCKEFELLER CENTER

Midtown Art Deco

ARCHITECTS
Raymond Hood, Godley &
Fouilhoux

COMPLETED
1939

*Despite the financial crisis
engulfing the nation, the
architects' ambitions were
visionary (TOP). John D.
Rockefeller Jr. (ABOVE)
ceremonially fixed the last
of 10 million rivets in
November, 1939, although
the RCA Building (RIGHT)
had opened in 1933.*

HIS OIL BUSINESS seemingly untouched by the Great Depression, John D. Rockefeller Jr., the world's richest man, had to keep spending if the robber baron image was not to overwhelm the family. And he loved opera. So why not the gesture of building a new home for the Metropolitan Opera?

There was a prime site in midtown Manhattan, not much to look at – its brownstones had been homes to speakeasies and cheap boarding houses during Prohibition – and it was something of an embarrassment to its owners, Columbia University. An opera house surrounded by hotels and office blocks could serve three motives: philanthropy, urban renewal, and profit. Rockefeller signed the lease for the tract between Fifth and Sixth Avenues and 48th and 51st Streets. The rent of $3,000,000 a year would be a third of the university's income.

But others were feeling the effect of the Depression, among them the benefactors of the opera house. The Met withdrew. In a brave and calculated decision, Rockefeller pressed on. The thinking became, opera is an old art, radio is the new. So, build a complex with the burgeoning Radio Corporation of America at its heart, then house other media interests – movies, press agencies, publishers. And make it a city within a city. The "largest construction project since the Pyramids" was under way, with more than 60 percent of its workforce coming from the vast pool of New York's unemployed.

There was little decoration to structural stonework at street level, to heighten the impact of reliefs, grand sculptures, and elaborate entrance framing. At the RCA Building (ABOVE), Lee Lawrie's bearded giant is flanked by side panels representing Sound and Light.

In contrast to the gold and glitter of Radio City Music Hall, the smaller Center Theater (RIGHT), on the south-west corner of the complex, featured somber mahogany. It did, though, boast a six-ton chandelier that required its own ventilation system to carry away the heat of 400 bulbs.

Diego Rivera's fresco for the lobby of the
RCA Building was destroyed when he
refused to paint out images of Lenin and
Marx. It was replaced by a Jose Maria
Sert mural (ABOVE) depicting, without
Communist overtones, the rewards of
physical and mental labor. Picasso and
Matisse turned down commissions there,
but Rockefeller Center was a rare, rich,
and welcome patron for American artists
during the Depression.

Rockefeller Center housed the world's first underground parking lot (ABOVE). Drivers waited in a comfortable lounge for their valet-parked cars to be brought to the surface, perhaps after an automated wash and polish (RIGHT). No delivery vehicles disturbed the complex's tranquility: they were routed down ramps into subterranean tunnels. Another, earlier innovation was the provision of observation windows in the fencing of the construction site. The legend is that it was John D. Rockefeller's idea, after a bossy supervisor waved him away from a hole in the fence where he was watching his own project take shape.

A "Tudor" English garden (ABOVE LEFT) was among 12 Gardens of the Nations (BELOW LEFT) on the 11th floor setback roof of the RCA Building.

Viewed from the sunken plaza – a café area in summertime, an ice rink in winter – the RCA Building's elegant setbacks emphasize its 70-story height (OVERLEAF). Its more slab-sided neighbors were planned and placed in a grouping that allowed open spaces, light, and air – as much as was consistent with maximizing rental income from the complex. The RCA Building is now the GE Building.

There were always lines round the block for
the Christmas show at Radio City Music
Hall, as here in 1944 (TOP), when the
movie was National Velvet. On their way
to the theater, visitors passed the world's
biggest Christmas tree, decorated with
20,000 lights. And for backing star
performers there were always the Rockettes
(ABOVE), the resident dance company,
accompanied by a 60-piece pit orchestra.

As the golden curtain rose in the world's
largest theater, a new movie would be
heralded by the sound of the world's largest
theater organ. Having abandoned the idea
of an opera house as the centepiece of the
complex, Rockefeller commissioned "a
palace for the people's pleasure." The most
brazenly Art Deco building in the
development, it seated 6,000 among
shimmering surfaces of bakelite and
aluminum, chrome, and crystal. Radio City
Music Hall always had sell-out crowds and
was the only unit in the complex to be
profitable from the beginning.

In the 1970s, Radio City Music Hall was scheduled for the wrecker's ball. Annual audiences down to 2 million were half the number required to balance the books. One problem was a decline in the number of wholesome Hollywood movies suited to the "family entertainment" promise of the theater's stage/screen presentations; television's home appeal was another. But public outcry and donations saved Radio City. It was designated a landmark. The superlative features of the 1930s — the world's largest cinema screen, the heaviest proscenium arch, the largest orchestra pit, the giant Wurlitzer, the elevating stage that inspired aircraft carrier design — were all to be preserved. It was to be another 20 years before the much-needed makeover took place. Ceilings were regilded with gold leaf (ABOVE LEFT); Ezra Winter's mural The Fountain of Youth above the grand stairway was restored (LEFT). The rounded ceiling of narrowing, overlapping bands glowed again from the lights hidden in the arches, above the 6,200 reupholstered seats.

CROTON AQUEDUCT

Working on the water

ENGINEER-DESIGNER
John B. Jervis

COMPLETED
1842

The High Bridge, the first of the city's major bridges, carried Croton water over the Harlem River (ABOVE LEFT). Its arches interfered with navigation and a single steel span replaced it in the 1920s.

Central Park was built around the receiving reservoir (LEFT). The water was distributed from a sturdy structure on Fifth Avenue (ABOVE).

BROOKS, PONDS, AND SPRING-FED wells supplied the city's water, bucketful by bucketful, until well into the 19th century. Tea Water Spring, near present-day Chinatown, was thought to be the purest supply and its output was hawked from water carts to the richer residences. But soon there was not enough water to clean the streets or put out the fires, and the sources were becoming polluted. A cholera epidemic that killed 3,000 in 1832 and the fire of 1835 that razed 20 blocks before it could be contained galvanized concerns.

The answer lay 50 miles north of Manhattan, well beyond the farming suburbs, where high and handsome lakes of crystal clear water were fed by the Croton River, a tributary of the Hudson. West of the village of Mt. Kisco, the Croton Dam was built of granite, and tunneling began: military prudence dictated that the aqueduct be underground, impervious to shellfire from any hostile warships that might venture up the Hudson.

In as straight a line as the engineers could manage, the aqueduct passed Sing Sing, Tarrytown, and Yonkers, and bridged the Harlem River to enter the city near 180th Street, then onto a receiving reservoir that was later to be a feature of Central Park. Distribution of water through the city was from a fortress-like reservoir at Fifth Avenue and 42nd Street, now the site of the New York Public Library

A city noted for its civic celebrations put on its biggest show ever for the opening, on July 4, 1842, although the party was muted by the newly powerful temperance organizations who insisted that only water, Croton water, be served to City Hall's guests.

Even the Croton's torrents, and a second aqueduct to channel them, would fail to quench the city's growing thirst. Supplies from the Catskill Mountains were turned on in 1917, and from the Delaware River in 1937.

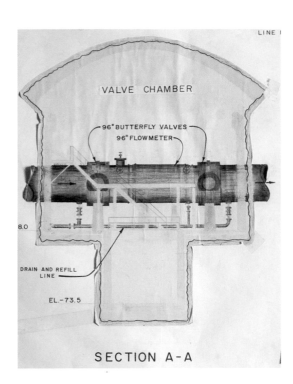

SECTION A-A

Croton water was inadequate for the city's needs almost as soon as the valves first opened, and even now summer droughts threaten water shortages. The engineering drawing (ABOVE) and the actuality of the pipework involved (RIGHT) were part of 1980s work on a third tunnel for water from the Hillview Reservoir, north of the city in Yonkers. When the reservoir system is full, it holds more than 5 billion gallons. Less than 10 percent of the city's water now comes from the Croton supply.

"No gentleman will live on a mere shelf under a common roof." That was a typical reaction to the Stuyvesant, America's first apartment block (ABOVE). *By the time the building was demolished, in 1957, most New Yorkers lived that way.*
RICHARD MORRIS HUNT, 1869

APARTMENT BUILDINGS

Sharing a roof in style

THE CITY'S TENEMENTS, absorbing wave after wave of poor immigrants into airless, waterless, lightless squalor, gave the notion of multi-unit housing a bad name. But in the late 1860s, Richard Morris Hunt, the Beaux Arts architect favored by the wealthy mansion builders, brought a new image to the concept. His five-story Stuyvesant Apartments on East 18th Street, the site of the first governor's fruit farm, offered spacious, civilized accommodation for 20 families, under one roof.

Living in purpose-built apartments was under way. Middle-class families faced with the rising costs of buying and running row houses could share amenities, and the expenses of living in space and style. The realtors' pitch was "why live in a row house when you can revel in the space of a noble building?" They coined the name "French flats," in recognition of their European origin, but soon the actuality was as grand as the promise and even the wealthiest New Yorkers took to the apartment way of life. The hotel architect Henry Hardenbergh filled the entire 55th–56th streets block on Seventh Avenue with the sumptuous Vancorlear apartment building, and followed it with the Dakota (1884) which, a century later, would receive unfortunate international notice when ex-Beatle John Lennon was murdered there, on his own doorstep.

The Dakota grew to eight stories on Central Park West at 72nd Street, a lonely yellow brick monster far north and west of fashionable areas (its name came from the jibe that it was so remote it was almost in Dakota). At first, it towered above shacks and smallholdings, but Central Park became a more agreeable outlook.

Rival developers, stung by the claim that this was the world's

Setbacks required by the building code allow these tenants balconies, plantings, and garden furniture (RIGHT). Bland designs and shoddy construction after World War II made the older, grander blocks the most desirable.

*Two towers allow more rooms with a
view at the San Remo, on Central Park
West* (LEFT AND ABOVE). *The architect,
Emery Roth, is credited with staunching
the flight to the suburbs of wealthy
New Yorkers when new highways
offered them access to greener pastures.
His several apartment buildings were
the height, literally and qualitatively,
of gracious inner-city living.*
EMERY ROTH, 1928

largest apartment block, set out to beat it for size, and splendor. Nearby, on Broadway, the 17-story, Beaux Arts Ansonia took the title in 1904, with 2,500 rooms shared among 350 tenants, who had their own swimming pool. Then the Astors exploited a piece of their landholdings by building the Apthorp, an Italian Renaissance palazzo of 12 stories with carriage entrances to a courtyard where fountains played. The Belnord, on Broadway and 86th Street, had apartments of up to 14 rooms and a trade entrance leading underground so that residents would not be disturbed by deliveries.

Servants lived in the attics, and mail arrived by pneumatic tube, posted by concierges in the lavish lobbies. Later buildings had one enormous apartment on each floor, and the attic areas were incorporated into the most fashionable spaces of all, the penthouses. The developer Donald Trump was still building for the extravagant end of the market in the 1980s while apartment dwelling had long since become the natural way of life for more modest New Yorkers. The form of leases would change so that tenants became owners, in "co-operatives" where they had the right to vet new neighbors in the buildings, sometimes withholding approval on questionable social and racial grounds.

REFINING THE CONCEPT

THE WORLD'S LARGEST APARTMENT BLOCK WHEN IT OPENED, THE DAKOTA HOUSED FEWER THAN 70 FAMILIES (AND THEIR SERVANTS, IN THE ATTIC), BUT EACH UNIT HAD UP TO 20 ROOMS.
Henry J. Hardenbergh, 1884

THE DECORATIVE ANSONIA ON THE WEST SIDE SERVED FREQUENT VISITORS TO NEW YORK. ITS SOUND-PROOFING ATTRACTED SINGERS AND MUSICIANS, FROM CARUSO TO TOSCANINI.
Paul E. M. Duboy, 1904

THE STRETCH OF BROADWAY AROUND 70TH
STREET WAS KNOWN AS THE BOULEVARD
WHEN THE DORILTON WAS BUILT; THUS THE
FRENCH INFLUENCE IN ITS DESIGN.
Janes & Leo, 1902

THE PETER STUYVESANT APARTMENT BUILDING
ON RIVERSIDE DRIVE, ONE OF SEVERAL BUILT
TO TAKE ADVANTAGE OF A LOCATION THAT
OVERLOOKED THE HUDSON.
William L. Rouse, 1912

BY THE 1920S, NEW YORKERS WERE COMMITTED
TO APARTMENT LIVING. TUDOR CITY ROSE
BETWEEN FIRST AND SECOND AVENUES: ITS 12
BUILDINGS CONTAINED 3,000 APARTMENTS.
Fred F. French, H. Douglas Ives, 1928

CENTRAL PARK IS ACROSS THE STREET FROM
THE TOWERS OF THE BERESFORD, ANOTHER OF
THE GRAND BLOCKS BUILT IN THE 1920S THAT
REVITALIZED THE UPPER WEST SIDE.
Emery Roth, 1929

Serving the city's guests

AN 1870s GUIDEBOOK counted more than 600 hotels in the city; 50, it advised, were well known, but only a couple of dozen were fashionable. One of those was the Astor House Hotel, designed in the Greek Revival style for John Jacob Astor as he set about monopolizing New York real estate. Built in the 1830s on Broadway between Barclay and Vesey streets, it had grand public rooms for political and cultural occasions, and water pumped even to the top, fifth, floor. At 23rd Street, the Fifth Avenue Hotel, on the site of an earlier inn and stagecoach stop, boasted fireplaces in every bedroom and a steam-powered elevator, the first in a hotel.

By the 1890s, steel-frame construction and electric elevators were enabling new hotels to be taller and taller, with room rates higher the higher the floor. Electric lighting, room service ordered by telephone, ice water on tap, and private bathrooms became the selling points. Hotels were built to serve the out-of-town shoppers who came to window gaze along Ladies' Mile,

Exploiting land their patriarch John Jacob compulsively bought, the Astors built one hotel after another. The 700-room Astor on Long Acre Square, now Times Square, is seen (RIGHT) *during a 1909 civic celebration. It was demolished before the introduction of landmark laws that might have saved it.*
CLINTON & RUSSELL, 1903

The Astors' arbored roof garden (ABOVE), *a block-long oasis of gazebos, fountains, and exotic plantings, was one of the city's most fashionable meeting places. Nine U.S. presidents were among the great and the good* (ABOVE RIGHT) *served from a vast kitchen and a vaulted wine cellar.*

"Peacock Alley" in the old Waldorf-Astoria – another parade ground for the city's fashionistas (PAGES 146–147).

and the countless salesmen supplying the new department stores. There were hotels for bachelors, and others for ladies only. Some served as gentlemen's clubs, others as marble-and-gold palaces for balls and banquets. Prosperous visitors from the provinces could name-drop fixed addresses in the city by renting suites in apartment hotels.

Soon traffic noise from the commercialism creeping north drove the rich from their residences on Lower Fifth Avenue. Two feuding cousins of the Astor family, William Waldorf Astor and John Jacob Astor IV, rebuilt their parents' mansions as hotels and combined them into the Waldorf-Astoria; legend has it that

THE McALPIN IN HERALD SQUARE, ANOTHER HOTEL BRIEFLY CLAIMING, IN 1912, TO BE THE WORLD'S LARGEST. IT HAD A NOTED DINING ROOM.
F. M. Andrews, 1912

ONE OF SEVEN HOTELS PLANNED FOR "TERMINAL CITY" AROUND GRAND CENTRAL, THE BILTMORE HAD 1,000 ROOMS WITH A VIEW.
Warren & Wetmore, 1913

THE RITZ TOWER, PARK AVENUE AND 57TH STREET, OPENED IN 1926 AS AN APARTMENT HOTEL, RENTING SUITES ON ANNUAL LEASES.
Emery Roth, Carrère & Hastings, 1926

THE HOTEL DELMONICO ON PARK AVENUE REVIVED A NAME RENOWNED IN SOCIETY CIRCLES: THAT OF DELMONICO'S RESTAURANT, CLOSED BY PROHIBITION.
Goldner & Goldner, 1928

GRAND CENTRAL RAILROAD TRACKS RUN BETWEEN FOUNDATIONS SUPPORTING THE COMMODORE. DONALD TRUMP LATER ENCASED IT IN GLASS.
Warren & Wetmore, 1919

INDIANA LIMESTONE AND GREEN ISLAND GRANITE CLAD THE ELEGANT, 14-STORY HOTEL MANHATTAN ON MADISON AVENUE AND 42ND STREET.
Henry J. Hardenbergh, 1896

THE SECOND HOTEL ON A COVETED FIFTH
AVENUE SITE, THE PLAZA, ONCE THE
CITY'S MOST EXPENSIVE HOTEL, IS STILL
ITS BEST KNOWN.
Henry J. Hardenbergh, 1907

THE NEW YORKER, BUILT TO SERVE PENN
STATION TRAVELERS, MADE IMAGINATIVE
USE OF THE SETBACK REQUIREMENTS OF
ZONING LAWS.
Sugarman & Berger, 1930

*The old Waldorf-Astoria (ABCVE) made way for the Empire
State Building. The present one (BELOW) occupies an entire city
block on Park Avenue. The two 625-ft.-high spires top private
apartments.* SCHULTZE & WEAVER, 1931

where the two units connected there were doors
that could be locked should the family tensions
boil over. With 1,300 rooms and 40 lavishly
appointed public areas, it was the city's grandest
hotel at the turn of the century.

Higher and bigger was the New York style:
1,000 rooms at the Biltmore, 2,000 at the
Commodore, both serving travelers to the new
Grand Central Terminal; 2,200 at the
Pennsylvania. In the 1920s, guests from Europe
disembarked from the great liners to find the
same standards of luxury at hotels boasting staff-
guest ratios of one-to-one. The second Waldorf-
Astoria opened on Park Avenue in 1931,
restoring the brand name to its former eminence.

Two historic theaters made way for the circular Marriott Marquis Hotel (LEFT) on Broadway at 45th Street. It did, however, incorporate a new theater. The hotel presaged the physical and social renewal of the Times Square area. Visitors checked in on the eighth floor, remote from the surrounding sleaze.
JOHN PORTMAN, JR., 1985

Twenty years earlier, the New York Hilton (ABOVE AND RIGHT) was built in anticipation of the 1964 New York World's Fair. Its tower, 400 ft. long and 400 ft. wide, is faced with blue glass windows of 2,200 rooms. The Hilton was one of the city's first convention hotels, equipped to serve large gatherings of like-minded executives.
WILLIAM B. TABLER, 1963

THE GRAND MANSIONS

Keeping up with the Astors

NEW YORK'S reason for being was the pursuit of wealth. And those who had it flaunted it by commissioning grand homes, side-by-side and competitively. The chosen showground in the late 19th century was a stretch of Fifth Avenue, north of Madison Square. The favored architect was Richard Morris Hunt, who had trained at the Ecole des Beaux Arts in Paris, and the favorite style was French chateau.

The Vanderbilt heirs, who had been excluded from New York society while Cornelius, the coarse, vulgarian founder of the dynasty, was alive, built mansions side by side on Fifth, with William K. Vanderbilt indulging his Alabama-born, French-educated wife with a $3 million chateau on the corner of 52nd Street.

Two branches of the Astor family also built adjacent palaces, at 34th Street. When a family feud opened up, William Waldorf Astor snubbed his neighbor, his Aunt Caroline, the legendary queen of New York Society, by demolishing his home and building an overshadowing hotel in its place. Her response was to move north, commissioning Richard Morris Hunt to build her a new palace at 65th Street, with pastoral views across the enforced naturalness of Central Park.

Tycoons who had made their fortunes elsewhere felt the need for a New York presence and residence: Carnegie and Frick, rich from Pittsburgh steel, and the Armour family, meat-packers from Chicago. William A. Clark, a copper miner from Montana, built the city's most expensive home, for $5 million, on the corner of 77th Street and Fifth Avenue in 1910. Lesser merchants peeked at the park from elegant townhouses on the cross streets. The mansion-owners considered them "cave-dwellers."

When his father died, leaving him $67 million, Cornelius Vanderbilt II marked his elevation to head of the family by rebuilding his already sumptuous home on Fifth Avenue at 57th Street. He demolished neighboring brownstones to gain a full block's frontage on the avenue (LEFT). Rich materials from around the world brought splendor to the interior: tropical mahogany, white Caen marble, ivory, mother-of-pearl. The Bergdorf Goodman store now occupies the site.
GEORGE B. POST, 1882

Charles M. Schwab, rich from Pittsburgh steel, went west, to Riverside Drive (RIGHT), to find space for 75 rooms, 40 baths, a marble pool, a bowling alley, and a pipe organ.
MAURICE HÉBERT, 1907

An Astor residence on Fifth
Avenue at 65th Street
(ABOVE). The Astors were
leaders among the mansion
builders. In one, the ballroom
had space for 400 guests, giving
rise to the name, "the Four
Hundred," to identify New
York's social aristocracy.
RICHARD MORRIS
HUNT

Jay Gould, financial speculator
and truly a "robber baron," was
shunned by New York society
and blackballed from the elite
clubs. Nevertheless, he had a
Fifth Avenue home (RIGHT)
at 47th Street.
STEPHEN D. HATCH, 1869

The railroad magnate Collis P. Huntington lived here, at Fifth Avenue and 57th Street (RIGHT). A family living in such a place would have quarters for up to 30 live-in servants.
OGDEN CODMAN, JR., 1902

Charles L. Tiffany, the jeweler, drew a detailed sketch of the house he wanted on Madison Avenue at 72nd Street. The house was built with brick facings in various shades of brown (BELOW). Tiffany's son, the artist Louis Comfort Tiffany, designed much of the interior, in styles ranging from "Old Dutch" to proto-Art Nouveau.
STANFORD WHITE, 1885

American-Victorian taste reflected in the homes of Madame de Barrios (ABOVE), the Havemayer family (ABOVE RIGHT), and August Heckscher (BELOW RIGHT). Wealthy clients hired decorating firms such as Louis Comfort Tiffany's Tiffany Studios to design interiors, and looked to events such as the 1876 Philadelphia Centennial Exhibition for influences. "More is better" was the style, and it was fashionable to show that the patron or the designer had scoured the world for treasures.

GENTLEMEN'S CLUBS

Mansions for members only

COMFORTABLE CLUBHOUSES where influential men relax in the company of like-minded companions have a long tradition in London. When New York took to the idea, the pioneers were the usual suspects from the city's elite – J. P. Morgan, the Vanderbilts, the Astors and the like; and they used their favored, fashionable architects, Stanford White and Charles McKim in particular.

J. P. Morgan commissioned White to build a home for the Metropolitan Club, which purported to be the most exclusive of all, alongside Central Park at 60th Street. It opened in 1894; the $2 million cost covered a discreet basement dining-room for members' wives, where Mrs. Vanderbilt, Mrs. Whitney, and Mrs. Roosevelt might monitor the quality of the food going upstairs.

The Metropolitan's design was labeled Florentine palazzo, and classical Italian became the favored style for grand clubhouses. The University Club on West 54th Street disguised its height with high arched windows suggesting just three stories – Italianate proportions. College shields carved in marble decorate the façades; "Renaissance" frescoes and murals adorn the interior. The actor Edwin Booth bought an early Gothic Revival brownstone on Gramercy Park as a home for his club, the Players. Stanford White remodeled it in the Italian Renaissance style, to the surprise of the neighbors.

Booth's club was for theater people. At the Century Association (White and McKim again, on West 43rd Street),

The 700 founding members pledged the $2 million cost of the Metropolitan Club (LEFT). *Above the grand rooms are bedrooms on the top floor; there are bowling alleys in the basement.*
STANFORD WHITE, 1894

The Manhattan Club's marble-clad building on Fifth Avenue at 34th Street (RIGHT) *was originally the home of A. T. Stewart, the city's wealthiest retailer. His stores were known as the Marble Palace and the Iron Palace; they were the first buildings in the city to use those materials extensively.*
JOHN KELLUM, 1869

dinner table conversation revolved around the promotion of interest in the arts. Democratic Party activists gathered at the Manhattan Club. Ivy League alumni founded clubs for themselves. Charles McKim, himself ex-Harvard, used dark-red "Harvard brick" and echoed the university's buildings for the Harvard Club on West 44th Street. Its Harvard Hall was considered to be one of the city's most distinguished interiors. The Yale Club, again on 44th Street, is a short walk from Grand Central Terminal, at the end of the line from the New Haven campus.

Perhaps the most endearing relic of these good old days is also on 44th Street, where J. P. Morgan donated a plot of land to rehouse the New York Yacht Club. The architect, Whitney Warren, used the Parisian Beaux Arts style, setting the bay windows into carved replicas of the sterns of old Dutch warships. When the clubhouse opened in 1900, it was estimated that between them the members owned more than 100 sailboats capable of crossing oceans.

The handsome Harvard Club on West 44th Street (LEFT), completed in 1915, echoes the design of buildings on the university campus.
CHARLES McKIM

The eccentrically ornamented New York Yacht Club (LEFT BELOW), also on 44th Street, was a place of pilgrimage for the world's yachtsmen when it displayed the America's Cup, sailing's most coveted trophy – until 1983 when Australia won it, the first-ever American loss.
WHITNEY WARREN, 1900

After a century wandering around the city, the University of Pennsylvania's Club of New York finally settled in 44th Street – Clubhouse Row (RIGHT). In 1922, at an earlier home, the Penn Club received commentaries on Penn football games by "direct telegraph wire" from Franklin Field.
TRACY & SWARTWOUT, 1901

Damping down the flames

A feature of older, lower plateaux on the New York skyline are the butts that give buildings water pressure on even the highest floors (RIGHT). They are made of wood, coopered like beer barrels. If fire damages them, they dump their contents on the blaze below.

Equally emblematic of the old city are the fire escapes of residential buildings (BELOW RIGHT). The novelist Henry James depicted them as "a little world of bars and perches and swings for human squirrels and monkeys."

A THIRD OF THE CITY went up in smoke in 1776. A hundred buildings were razed in an 1811 outbreak. The great fire of 1835 that began in a Pearl Street warehouse destroyed 650 buildings; ten years later, in the same area, 340 buildings burned down in one night. Until gushing supplies from the Croton Aqueduct were turned on in 1845, the problem was lack of water; just hand-pumped trickles from streams, ponds, and wells served all the city's needs. (There had been a fireboat on the East River since 1800, but the meager reach of its hoses limited it to damping down waterfront warehouses.)

Even with Croton water, the city long remained a tinder box. Much of the new building was in less-combustible brick and stone, but wood was the cheaper construction material and landlords continued to use it for poor housing. Private and volunteer fire companies operated through an inefficient infrastructure, weakened by Tammany Hall corruption. In the last decade of the 19th century, more than 100 people died in tenement fires.

Two blazes caught the city's imagination and survive in its folklore. First, the Crystal Palace fire of 1858, when the sparkling centerpiece of the city's celebration of its own wondrous achievements collapsed, broiled over its own four acres of burning floorboards. As the iron framing melted and twisted, 15,000 panes of glass crashed into the inferno.

More tragic in terms of lives lost, the Triangle Shirtwaist Company fire of 1911 taught the city a lesson that it took profoundly to heart. At the time, New York industry employed 600,000 workers in 30,000 factories, mostly sewing garments, for 11 hours a day, six days a week. Triangle was one such sweatshop. When the fire started one winter Saturday afternoon, two floors of fabrics and cotton waste quickly became a deathtrap. The consequences were far-reaching, beyond mere fire precautions: limits on women's and children's working hours, legally enforced standards for factory conditions, disability compensation. State Assemblyman Al Smith would become New York's favorite politician as he overwhelmed vested interests to power through the reforms.

Jets from firehoses barely reach the afflicted floors of the Triangle Shirtwaist Company building on Washington and Greene Streets (LEFT). More than 140 women, some as young as 14, died here, the doors to their sweatshop locked on the outside. Many jumped to their deaths in groups, holding hands.

BROWNSTONES

Human scale among the towers

IT'S THE NAME OF A DARK RED SANDSTONE, an economical facing material quarried in nearby New Jersey, but "brownstone" came to be the generic name for New York row houses even when they were clad with brick or limestone, or the white marble quarried in Westchester, just to the north.

In the 1790s, in a city plagued by almost-daily fires among its wooden structures, ordinances decreed that new buildings of two stories or more should be of brick or stone. The frontages of the grid plan blocks began to fill from the south with solid, dignified dwellings. In 1825, there were 3,000 under construction.

The first architectural style was Federal, an essentially English expression of Classical traditions. The basic plan filled a building lot 25 ft. wide. A half-buried basement was dug out to allow for a service entrance, a dining room whose windows poked above street level at the front, and a kitchen at the back. The first, "parlor," floor was reached from the street by a flight of steps, the stoop, leading into a hallway alongside two living rooms, squarish in shape, separated by hinged or sliding doors that allowed the whole area to be opened up for entertaining. A stairway to the second floor led to two bedrooms, sometimes separated by a "pantry" where washstands and chamberpots would be stored. Every room had two windows and a wood-burning fireplace, although if there were a third floor for the servants its rooms would be less congenial.

In the early days of brownstones, landowners did not feel the need for architects. Teams of building craftsmen – cellar diggers, bricklayers, masons, and carpenters, working to drawings by a journeyman draftsman – replicated the restrained design block after block. Individual touches came from the ornamentation of doors and window frames and the ironwork of railings.

By the 1880s, when these photographs were
taken, Brooklyn, a working city in its own
right, was also well established as the nation's
first commuter suburb, where stylish people
found elegant homes. Builders chose the
ornamental ironwork, even the street lamps,
from makers' catalogs that changed in response
to the architectural style of the moment. It
was a more economical way of adding
distinguishing touches than carving in stone.
But "streetscape unity," not personalization,
was the goal.

Fashions changed. After the Federal style came Greek Revival, Gothic Revival, Italianate, Romanesque, Renaissance. Brownstones grew wider, taller, and grander as architects were commissioned to create one-off homes. Then, as now, location was crucial: in the late 1880s, a four-story brownstone on the Upper East Side might cost $60,000; a dwelling of the same specifications on Lower Eighth Avenue would be half the price. Some of the finest townhouses were built in Brooklyn, inspiring the claim that it was "the best built city in the country." But, perhaps wistful for the historic landmarks of older cities, poet Walt Whitman observed that "our architectural greatness consists in the hundreds and thousands of suburban private dwellings."

Controls imposed in the Upper East Side Historic District came too late to save this last relic of a brownstone row in the East 60s. The bland façades behind indicate what's to replace it.

Ohio stone was tried as a facing. Elevators were installed. Internal plumbing and mechanical heating systems came into use. In *Washington Square*, Henry James has a character advising a move uptown every three or four years, to the newer developments that had the latest improvements.

Brownstones were intended for the burgeoning middle classes, but over the years they have served most of the city's ethnic and economic groupings as the social status of neighborhoods fluctuated.. Single-family homes became tenements; tenements were graciously restored in urban renewal programs. The skyline of skyscrapers would come to symbolize the city; but the brownstones represent its humanity.

DEMOLITION

Burying the past, imperfectly

RELENTLESS RENEWAL became a Manhattan obsession. Madison Square Presbyterian Church, a masterpiece by McKim, Mead & White, stood for just seven years. Their admired Moorish Madison Square Garden lasted 35 years. St. John's Chapel, built in 1803 and considered one of the nation's finest specimens of church architecture, was gone by the end of World War I.

Theatrical legends died in the debris of the Roxy and the Ziegfeld. Grand hotels – the Murray Hill and the Ritz-Carlton – disappeared along with the ghosts of a golden age. Mansions and townhouses gracing Park and Fifth Avenues made way for apartment and office blocks. The city's largest private ballroom imploded as a Whitney residence was reduced to rubble.

What all these victims had in common, of course, was modest height. And if profit was to be squeezed out of every inch of dirt on this finite island, taller was better. Guilt about such wanton destruction surfaced in the early 1960s, but not enough to stop it. Demolition might begin on a Saturday, not normally a working day for unionized labor, so that by Monday morning, when lawyers' and municipal offices opened, a conservationist protest was too late. There was a sad society whose members roamed the ruins, buying fragments

THE CITY'S DEFENSES

Preserving peace, preparing for war

IN THE DAYS OF SAIL AND BROADSIDE, no seaport city had better natural protection against seaborne attack than New York. First, where the ocean was squeezed into the channel between Brooklyn and Staten Island, any enemy armada would be forced into close formation, within range of guns on the shores; it would then it would have to sail the long gauntlet across the Upper Bay.

Fort Hamilton commanded the Verrazano Narrows from the Brooklyn side, storing its ammunition on a one-acre reef, Fort Lafayette. On Staten Island, there was Fort Wadsworth, recalled in history books as the target of the last salvo of the Revolution, petulantly fired at by a retreating British man-o'-war. If any marauders had survived the crossfire to storm Manhattan, they would have been greeted by the cannons of Fort Jay and Castle Williams on Governors Island, just off the island's southern tip.

In attacking mode, New York's war efforts centered on the Brooklyn Navy Yard on Wallabout Bay. The warships that dispersed Barbary pirates were built here, as were those that preyed on British merchant shipping during the War of 1812. It became the world's largest shipyard – 300 acres and 70,000 workers – during the intense, 24/7 activity of World War II, building aircraft carriers and battleships, among them the *Missouri*, aboard which the Japanese surrender was taken in September 1945.

The 369th Regiment Armory on 142nd Street was built for the Harlem Hellfighters who fought in World War I as a unit of the French Army; segregation policies of the time prevented black enlisted men serving in U.S. battle groups. But the regiment was properly honored in the Fifth Avenue victory parade.
TACHAU & VOUGHT, 1924

Brooklyn Navy Yard, officially the New York Naval Shipyard (ABOVE), in 1946, winding down from the war during which its production had exceeded the whole of Japan's. Cold War needs kept it active until 1966.

A central atrium in Cass Gilbert's ingenious warehousing for the Brooklyn Army Terminal (BELOW RIGHT) allowed easy loading of supplies to all floors.

Nearby, in Sunset Park, the Brooklyn Army Terminal, built in 1919 by Cass Gilbert, architect of the Woolworth Building, served as the holding center for the three million troops who shipped out of New York for the Western campaigns of World War II. Both complexes made way for industrial parks.

But it was suspicion of the enemy within that inspired the city's most interesting defense buildings – armories. They were a response to the fears among established citizens when the draft riots of 1863 demonstrated the raw power of street mobs; and then there was the increasingly surly restiveness of poor immigrants suffering the privations of overcrowded tenements and economic depressions. Thus the idea of regiments based in fortresses that could withstand sieges seemed a comforting notion to the bourgeoisie. Around 30 armories were built in a 25-year period.

A block-long "French medieval" castle took shape on 94th Street between Madison and Park Avenues. A Mexican castle was copied on Sumner Avenue in Brooklyn. The flamboyant impregnability of towers, turrets, and crenellated battlements gave zero-tolerance warning to the streets. Kingsbridge Armory in the Bronx had the world's largest drill hall, 180,000 sq. ft. of marching space. At the 7th Regiment Armory on Park Avenue, officers relaxed in surroundings designed by Louis Comfort Tiffany.

Some armories were demolished, others are still National Guard bases. Yet others have become TV studios, exhibition centers, and shelters for the homeless.

AMERICAN MUSEUM OF NATURAL HISTORY

Astronomy to zoology in four blocks

AS THE SCOPE OF NATURAL SCIENCES studies has expanded, colliding with and overlapping other disciplines, New York's natural history museum has constantly extended its home, not always to pleasing architectural effect. Classical lettering over the original pink granite, column-flanked façade on 77th Street promises Truth, Knowledge, Vision; to fulfill the promise now requires the halls, workshops, theaters, libraries, and laboratories that fill four city blocks on the Upper West Side, from Central Park West to Columbus Avenue, from 77th Street up to 81st.

It was a brave decision to build here, so far north of the 1870's heart of the city, and the museum struggled at first. The then brash idea of Sunday opening helped, as did expeditions to Mongolia and Africa in search of human ancestors; discoveries made on them captured the imagination of the public and the city's school-children. Now the museum receives more than three million visitors a year, for whom the world-famous dinosaur exhibit is a principal attraction.

The most recent addition to the museum is the Rose Center for Earth and Space, a cube of glass containing an aluminum sphere that replaces the old Hayden Planetarium. Computers and lasers re-create cosmic effects, and there is a very real relic: a 15-ton meteorite that the museum acquired a century ago.
POLSHEK PARTNERSHIP, 2000

MUSEUM MILE

The avenue of treasures

THE BACKBONE OF NEW YORK'S POSTURE as the nation's cultural capital is a stretch of Fifth Avenue alongside Central Park. Its southern marker is a former Whitney mansion just south of 79th Street, bought and sensitively restored by the French government as a home for its cultural activities. (The French connection is not inappropriate; the American architects of several of the city's best-loved buildings drew inspiration from Paris's Ecole des Beaux Arts.) At the northern end, on the edge of East Harlem, the Museo del Barrio celebrates the art and culture of Latin America, acknowledging the heritage of its neighborhood.

Richard Morris Hunt designed
the Met's central Fifth Avenue
block; McKim, Mead & White
added the wings. Central Park's
designer, Frederick Law
Olmsted, expressed early
concerns that the Met would
encroach on his preserve — and
it has, to make way for such
treasures as the Federal period
bank façade, and a reassembled
Nile Valley temple (RIGHT).

In between, mansions built by 19th-century tycoons display the treasures their owners collected – and many, many more, acquired through endowments by family foundations, and further philanthropy. Visitors by the million now tread the mostly marble floors that once welcomed home Andrew Carnegie, Henry Clay Frick, both rich from steel and railroads, the industrialist William Starr Miller, and the financier Felix Warburg. Modern buildings in the name of Guggenheim and Whitney (one block

The grand columns of the Met's frontage (LEFT) are 800 years younger than those re-erected at the Museum's Cloisters branch in Fort Tryon Park (ABOVE).

east, on Madison Avenue) are further legacies from an era of explosive wealth creation, and an accompanying benevolence.

And across the street, in Central Park itself, the city's own Metropolitan Museum of Art overlooks it all, like a proud *grande dame*. Perhaps the most comprehensive, eclectic museum in the world, it owns more than three million objects for display in a constantly enlarging complex.

A family of three once lived in the 80-room Carnegie mansion at 91st Street. For its time, 1901, it was technologically advanced, with a steel-frame structure, an elevator, and primitive air conditioning – air blown across tanks of cool water. Now it is the Cooper-Hewitt National Design Museum (LEFT), part of the Smithsonian Institution. Its beginnings were a small applied arts museum founded by Peter Cooper, the inventor and entrepreneur. BABB, COOK & WILLARD, 1901

Henry Clay Frick was a partner of Carnegie's, in the world's largest steel business. A serious collector of painting and sculpture, Frick bequeathed his art and his 70th Street mansion (LEFT) to the city; the Frick Collection opened to the public in 1935. CARRERE & HASTINGS, 1914

Purpose-built to house "the city's family album," the Museum of the City of New York faces the park at 103rd Street (SECOND BOTTOM LEFT). With a pediment on Ionic columns, and red-brick facings trimmed with white marble, the building harks back to Georgian Colonial architecture.
JOSEPH H. FREEDLANDER, 1932

The widow of Felix M. Warburg, the financier, donated her home at 92nd Street to house the Jewish Museum (BOTTOM LEFT). Major redevelopment in the 1990s, doubling its exhibition space, used limestone from the original quarry.
C. P. H. GILBERT, 1908

Legend has it that the Metropolitan Museum spurned an offer of books from one of its most generous benefactors, the financier J. P. Morgan. Thus, the Pierpont Morgan Library is not on Museum Mile, but at East 36th Street. The magnificent East Room (RIGHT) displays books as early as a Gutenberg Bible of 1455.
MCKIM, MEAD & WHITE, 1906

WHITNEY MUSEUM OF AMERICAN ART

The upended ziggurat

ARCHITECT
Marcel Breuer & Assocs., with
Hamilton Smith

COMPLETED
1966

IT TOOK A WHILE FOR THE formidable Whitney building to gain the city's acceptance. Architectural commentators labeled it as "the most disliked building in New York." It was overbearing, threatening, "a Guggenheim with corners." Certainly, this virtually windowless block of gray granite was a startling new presence on the fashionable Upper East Side.

Contributing to the disquiet was the amiable, bohemian image of the Whitney collection. Gertrude Vanderbilt Whitney, heiress and sculptor, had first shown the work of young American artists at her own studio in Greenwich Village. In the 1920s, she offered her collection to the Metropolitan Museum, who rejected it. Piqued, she converted a row of old houses to create a cozy museum on 8th Street. Then there was a comfortable but inadequate home on 54th Street. Now this homely inheritance was confined to a fortress.

But with familiarity and use, Marcel Breuer's up-turned ziggurat gained respect, even affection. Art looked well on its rough-textured walls; there were the classy touches of teak and bronze trimmings. The outside might be bleak, but the inside became recognized as a proud setting for the most important collection of 20th-century American art. And perhaps Breuer had been right to say, "I didn't try to fit the building to its neighbors because the neighboring buildings aren't any good."

The Madison Avenue–75th Street corner is a small, awkward site for such a prestigious museum. To enter the Whitney, visitors cross a bridge over a moat containing a sculpture court.

Attached to concrete walls, an open
staircase of stone steps and teak handrails
serve the museum's three upper floors
(ABOVE). Expensive detailing gives the
somber interior its character. There are just
six windows in the 85-ft.-high north wall
(RIGHT), all angularly shaped and
seemingly arbitrarily placed.

SOLOMON R. GUGGENHEIM MUSEUM

Frank Lloyd Wright's concrete snail

ARCHITECT
Frank Lloyd Wright

COMPLETED
1959

SOLOMON R. GUGGENHEIM, hugely rich from his family's interest in mining and smelting, collected modern European art. In 1943 he commissioned Frank Lloyd Wright, the most famous architect of his day, to build a home for it, where New Yorkers could admire an unsurpassed collection of Kandinskys and works by, among others, Chagall, Modigliani, Leger, and Klee.

It was 16 years before the museum opened. World War II was long over before the city passed the plans; after all, approval was required for a spiral concrete snail to be parked on Fifth Avenue at the corner of 88th Street, not far from the formal splendor of the Metropolitan Museum. Wright, not noted for his humility, was bruised by the bureaucrats' doubts.

Then he battled with the museum's director over the interior; the outside spiral was to be repeated inside – a sloping ramp seven stories high, curving round a central atrium reaching from street level to the glass roof. In Wright's view, this offered an egalitarian way of viewing pictures; visitors would take the elevator to the top level and walk down and round, pausing as they wished, taking in the whole scene at all times. But, curators pleaded, there was not enough room for the pictures, this generous piece of prime real estate was providing precious little wall space.

Wright won all the arguments. But neither he nor Solomon Guggenheim lived to attend the 1959 opening of a museum that itself is as much of an attraction as its contents.

(ABOVE) *Frank Lloyd Wright. The Guggenheim was not his only spiral building; a gift shop in San Francisco used the same dynamic principle in 1948. He also left plans for a mile-high skyscraper, intended for Chicago.*

A top-heavy spiral in a neighborhood of rectangles, the Guggenheim (RIGHT) was one of few aesthetically ambitious buildings to arise in the city in the decades following World War II.

(LEFT) *A feeling of wide open space, an impression totally at odds with the traditional museum practice of leading the visitor from room to room.*

THE MUSEUM OF MODERN ART

Showing the new

ARCHITECTS
Philip L. Goodwin, Edward
Durell Stone
COMPLETED
1939

Yoshio Taniguchi
COMPLETED
2004

A DREAM OF THE 1930s had been to create a continuous cultural complex spreading north from Rockefeller Center. But there were sites in the way that not even the Rockefellers could acquire; thus the building they sponsored for the Museum of Modern Art appeared as an outpost, on 53rd Street.

Built in the early International Style, featuring reinforced concrete and glass, the museum provided a cool, serene showcase for the most renowned collection of modern art in the world. Over the years, as adjacent plots became available, architectural eminences like Philip Johnson and Cesar Pelli added wings, lobby space, galleries, and a garden, doubling the original space.

In 2001, MoMA took temporary quarters in Queens while the most expensive makeover in museum history took place, made possible by the acquisition of yet more space around its midtown home. In a

A new kind of façade punctuates 53rd Street in 1939 (LEFT). In the 2004 restoration, aluminum, black granite, and more glass clad the expanded spaces. The reframed entrance (BELOW) leads to the light and height of an indoor boulevard through to 54th Street.

In the 2004 renovation (LEFT), the garden has grown, and new walls on 54th Street are strategically perforated to give surprising views of MoMA's neighbors.

Barnett Newman's Broken Obelisk *in the new second floor atrium* (ABOVE). *On the sixth floor, space for a 100-ft.-wide painting,* F-111 *by James Rosenquist* (RIGHT). *Despite the addition of 40,000 sq. ft. of exhibition space, MoMA can still show only a tiny proportion of its holdings at any one time.*

throwback to the great age of private benefaction, the trustees personally contributed almost two-thirds of the $850 million budget. Through an entrance lobby covering 12,000 sq. ft., around an atrium 100 ft. high, visitors now find six floors of white display walls with 40 acres of oak flooring underfoot.

At the 2004 reopening, the new MoMA was greeted as the city's "most exquisite work of art for a generation." The private donors' names are etched on frosted glass in the atrium. The admission charge is $20, thought to be the highest museum entrance fee in the world.

DEPARTMENT STORES

The temples of temptation

IT WAS KNOWN AS LADIES' MILE, a glittering corridor of store frontages along Sixth Avenue between 10th and 23rd streets and spilling over on to Broadway, arranged to attract the prosperous residents of Fifth Avenue. At the heart of it was the dry goods emporium of R. H. Macy, a former whaling captain, which opened for business in 1858. Nearby, Alexander Turney Stewart gathered together under one roof displays of merchandise that had previously required visits to several specialty shops. Thus the department store was born, as was the phrase "window shopping." Amid lavish architecture of brick and terracotta, marble and glass, the conspicuous consumption of mass production was underway.

New concepts in retailing – clearance sales, a Christmas shopping season, money-back guarantees – were refined here. By the turn of the century, shopping in New York was assuming its modern, addictive form, a leisure pastime rather than a necessary chore. That encouraged the Straus brothers, the new owners of Macy's, to build the world's largest department store, with 10 acres of selling space, at Herald Square. Other big names – Gimbel Brothers, Lord & Taylor, B. Altman – followed them north; later still midtown Fifth Avenue became the showcase for elegant shopping.

Department stores still anchor New York shopping but, heading uptown on Madison Avenue, a new generation of small boutiques and specialty stores now provide retail therapy along a less overwhelming ladies' mile.

The chore of shopping turned into pleasurable outings with friends and retailers began to lay out their wares as counter displays among which women could wander – and wonder. Another feature of the new retailing was fixed, marked prices, saving the embarrassment of bargaining.

Styles of the 60s reflected in Saks 34th Street store (OVERLEAF). Earlier, in 1924, the founder's son established Saks Fifth Avenue, beside St. Patrick's Cathedral, to serve a more affluent uptown market.

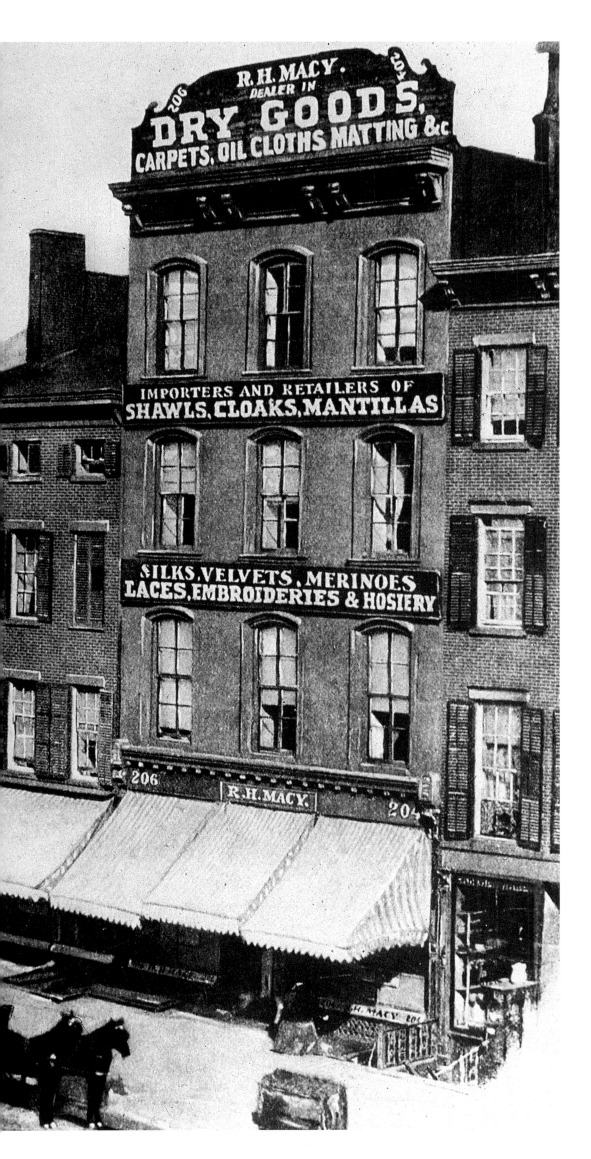

Macy's first store. on Sixth Avenue, quickly became one of the city's show places (LEFT). *By 1881, it had arc lighting, cash-carrying pneumatic tubes, and telephones. Macy claimed that it was the world's largest store, a title that could certainly be applied to its Herald Square successor* (BELOW). *This was the first large store to open north of Ladies' Mile.*
DELEMOS & CORDES, 1902

"What cannot be
found here is not to
be found in any
shopping district
anywhere."

KING'S HANDBOOK
OF NEW YORK,
1893

Siegel-Cooper's, on Sixth Avenue at 18th Street (TOP LEFT), was at the heart of Ladies' Mile, claiming to sell "everything under the sun." It was mobbed on its opening day in 1896, and the marble terrace on the main floor where a fountain played among colored lights became a favorite meeting place. In World War I, the building became, briefly, a military hospital.

DELEMOS & CORDES, 1896

B. Altman's move north to a site among the fine houses on Fifth Avenue distressed the neighbors, so Benjamin Altman gave his store the flourishes of a Florentine palazzo and omitted external signage (TOP MIDDLE). As other retailers established themselves nearby, the wealthy residents moved farther up the avenue. Altman's closed in 1989.

TROWBRIDGE & LIVINGSTON, 1906

The Gimbel brothers, sons of a Bavarian-born peddler, had opened stores in the Midwest before building their Manhattan store (TOP RIGHT) just a block away from Macy's. The rivalry between the two giants became a feature of New York retailing. But Gimbel's did not survive; in the 1980s the building was gutted, refaced in glass, and became a shopping mall.

D.H. BURNHAM, 1912

Simpson, Crawford & Simpson remodeled its Sixth Avenue store to distinguish it as more up-market than its neighbors (LEFT). Large windows allowed by the black-painted, gold-decorated, cast-iron framework displayed merchandise without price tags – a conceit returned to a century later by high-class retailers.

THOMAS STENT, 1879

Bloomingdale's began as a lonely uptown dry goods store. As the Third Avenue elevated railroad brought brought more and more customers to its doors, "Bloomies" grew and grew, finally filling the 59th-60th Streets block across to Lexington Avenue, now the main showcase for its window displays. By the 1970s, it was the city's trendiest store, the place where New York shoppers "danced chic to chic."

STARRETT & VAN VLECK, 1930

Not to be outdone by its glitzy commercial neighbors, the stores of Fifth Avenue, St. Patrick's lights up for Christmas in this 1930s display. The twin spires are 330 ft. high. Now closely surrounded, the situation in 1875 (RIGHT) seems almost rural.

ST. PATRICK'S CATHEDRAL

A fashionable address for the faithful

ARCHITECT
James Renwick, Jr.

COMPLETED
1878

A PROTESTANT MOB THREATENED to burn down the first St. Patrick's Cathedral, set as it was on the frontline of 19th-century racial and religious tensions. At the center of the storm was the incumbent bishop, John Hughes, a powerful, streetwise, politically savvy advocate of Catholic causes. Appointed archbishop in 1850, he quickly announced plans for a new St. Patrick's, well north of the social flashpoints. The site was a piece of land the church owned at Fifth Avenue and 50th Street; the intention had been to create a peaceful, rural cemetery here, but gravediggers' shovels hit New York bedrock just below the surface.

The cornerstone of architect James Renwick's granite and marble, Gothic-style cathedral was laid in August 1858, and construction, interrupted by the Civil War, continued for 21 years, at a final cost twice the original estimate. Architectural scholars see in the façade strong influences from Germany's medieval Cologne Cathedral (whose towering spires were actually built at the same time as those of St. Patrick's). Over the years, renewals and additions like the great rose window and bronze doors to Fifth Avenue have marked the reigns of the cardinal archbishops, who have made the cathedral a focal point for the nation's Catholic faithful.

The original St. Patrick's, on Mott and Prince streets, did indeed burn down, though not at the hands of arsonists. It was rebuilt as a parish church.

PLACES OF WORSHIP

Sanctuary in the city

IN NEW YORK, THE CATHEDRALS and churches reached for the heavens in styles that echoed Rome, Chartres, and the abbeys and minsters of medieval England. The idioms of Classical, Byzantine, Gothic, and Renaissance architecture were used.

The names concerned, the benefactors and builders, were, however, very much those of hustling New York. Rockefellers and Vanderbilts, whose antecedents had bought city plots at inconsequential prices, generously wrote off the inflation of values, enabling congregations to find the peace of God in the city. An Astor paid for the bronze doors of Trinity Church; J. P. Morgan's contribution of $500,000 helped solve engineering problems at St. John the Divine. The architects, too, were from the upper registers: the men of mansion-building and power statements in stone: McKim, Mead & White, Richard Morris Hunt.

In another reference to an old European tradition – places of worship

Trinity Church's slim elegance bestows visual power despite the overwhelming presence of its Wall Street neighbors (ABOVE). Queen Anne's 1705 grant of land to the Protestant parish gave it continuing title to much of lower Manhattan.
RICHARD UPJOHN, 1846

The nave of the world's largest Episcopalian cathedral takes form in the 1920s (ABOVE, RIGHT) on a site dominating the Morningside Heights plateau. The erratic progress of St. John the Divine was caused by 50 years of mind-changing about its design, and consequential shortages of funds. When work stopped for World War II, the dollar count was already at 20 million.
HEINS & LA FARGE, UNTIL 1911; CRAM & FERGUSON, 1942

Gothic conceits wrap the steel frame of Riverside Church, a neighbor of Grant's Tomb on Riverside Drive (LEFT). John D. Rockefeller's support for the free-thinking pastor, Dr. Harry Emerson Fosdick, changed its religious allegiance from Baptist to liberal interdenominational. The architectural references to the great cathedrals of northern France continue inside (RIGHT). White Caen stone, stained glass made in Chartres and Reims, and a carillon of 74 bells reflect the Rockefeller generosity.
ALLEN, PELTON & COLLENS, 1929

whose construction persists long after the generations who began it, like Cologne Cathedral completed in 1880, some 632 years after it was started, and Gaudi's still ongoing Sagrada Familia in Barcelona – New York has the Cathedral Church of St. John the Divine, started in 1892, still under construction.

Many among the millions disembarking at Ellis Island had made the journey to escape religious persecution; their inbred fears led to discreet places of worship – homes and "storefront" churches, with just a few benches behind shrouded windows. Early Jewish arrivals practiced their faith that way, but were soon important enough to the life of the city to establish distinct congregations and synagogues – more than 20 by the mid-19th century.

Huguenot refugees built L'Eglise du St. Esprit on Church Street; the tiny Church of St. Nicholas opened in 1820 to serve the Greek Orthodox arrivals. Harlem's African-Americans, mostly Baptist, built the world's largest church of that denomination – the Abyssinian Baptist Church, of which Adam Clayton Powell Jr, would become pastor.

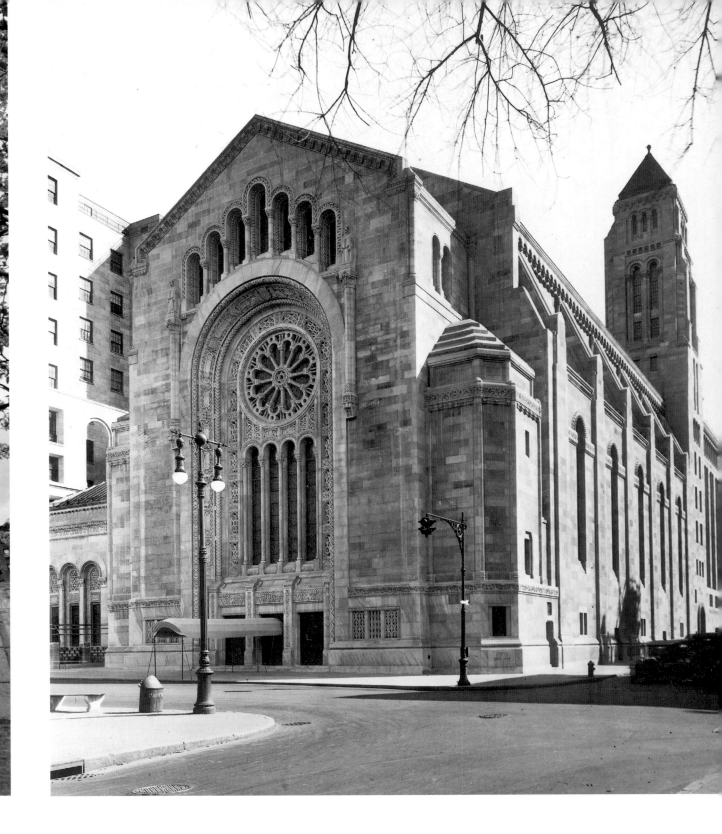

Delegates and staff posted to the United Nations from Muslim countries founded the Islamic Cultural Center, and went on to build the mosque (ABOVE LEFT), facing Mecca at Third Avenue and 96th Street. There are many more mosques in the city, most of them not purpose-built, but ad hoc assemblies in homes, community centers, and disused commercial buildings. The first record of a New York Muslim organization is at the end of the 19th century.
SKIDMORE, OWINGS & MERRILL, 1991

The largest synagogue built in modern times stands at the corner of Fifth Avenue and 65th Street. Temple Emanu-El (ABOVE) seats 2,500 in a 100-ft.-high nave, bathed in a glow of light from the façade windows – stained glass in a great rose, and in rows of lancets above and below. The temple is home to the oldest Reform Jewish congregation in the city, founded by German immigrants in 1845.
ROBERT D. KOHN; CHARLES BUTLER; CLARENCE STEIN; MAYERS, MURRAY & PHILIP, 1929

CONEY ISLAND

"The Empire of the Nickel"

THE MOMENTUM began soon after the Civil War with fashionable hotels and a racetrack offering weekend solace for Brooklyn's finest. Then the railroads got there, and the subway, and Coney Island's honky-tonk heyday was underway. Soon the thoroughbreds to be bet on were prize fighters rather than horses, lunch ceased to be silver service, but became a 5 cent sausage in a bun – the hot dog was invented here – and every weekend was carnival time.

Behind a broad, white, two-mile beach, later extended, and a boardwalk, dream machines arose among hundreds of peep shows and pop stands: Steeplechase Park (1897), where wooden horses raced along iron rails; Luna Park (1903), for a Trip to the Moon in a darkened theater; and Dreamland (1904), where Roman gladiators drove chariots through triumphal arches.

Vesuvius erupted nightly. Pompeii burned. Cleopatra was ravished. New York's huddled masses found the canals of Venice, Japanese villages, and Eskimo settlements at the end of a 5-cent subway ride. In its prime, the world's greatest amusement park attracted 20 million visitors a year.

Times and tastes changed. After World War II, New Yorkers sought quieter weekends, and Robert Moses had built more tranquil beachfront parks, with the parkways to reach them. Parts of Coney Island declined to ghetto status. One attraction that remains is the New York Aquarium, which also houses serious research facilities.

New "mechanical amusements" made their first public appearances at Coney Island. The lady onlooker in 1903 (LEFT) would have needed to avoid sidewalk air jets designed to lift her petticoats. Attendance on a summer Sunday often reached 1 million (RIGHT).

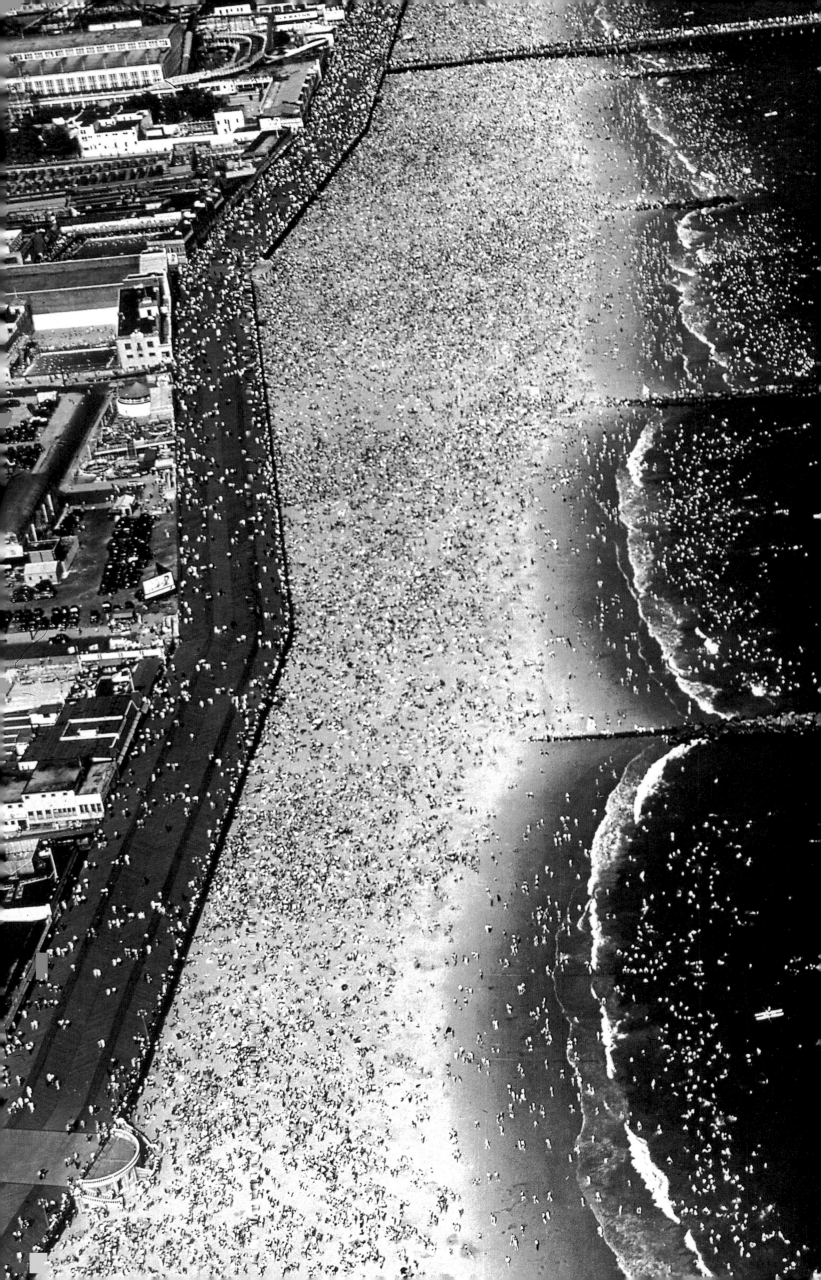

At a time when many of its visitors lived in homes without electricity,
Luna Park (LEFT AND ABOVE) boasted 250,000 light bulbs. Its rival
attraction, Dreamland, claimed to have 1 million. Luna Park was
designed by the theater architect, Frederic Thompson. It burned down in
1944, marking the beginning of the end of Coney Island's glory days.

THE THEATER DISTRICT

The great white way

SHOW BUSINESS HAS ALWAYS clung to Broadway. It began down at the Bowery end, where a cluster of minstrel theaters and taverns shared the aura of the country's largest auditorium, the Great Bowery Theater (1826). As people who could afford theater tickets moved north, so did their entertainment, making sporadic leaps up Broadway. In the late 19th century, the bandwagon stopped at Times Square, and it has been there ever since.

The first electric signs began to sparkle; where Broadway collides with Seventh Avenue, the *New York Times* girdled its headquarters with the day's headlines spelled out in light bulbs. It was a natural gathering place, a crossroads of the rapid transit system, with Grand Central Terminal just to the east. Here was passing trade for theater and burlesque, cabarets and dance halls. As the lively arts are night-time entertainment, they bathed themselves in light – by the megawatt. The Great White Way was created.

The composer Oscar Hammerstein built three theaters in Times Square; by the 1920s, 60 more vied for attention on the side streets; 42nd Street was the location of choice for the impresarios, although there were full houses as far north as 50th Street. Songwriters sold their work in Tin Pan Alley – not a place, but a concept named for the tinny sound of audition pianos. Gossip writers tracked down stars and showgirls at Sardi's and Lindy's restaurants.

Then the movie theaters came to dominate the entertainment mix. And it was the movies that would nudge live theater into

PRECEDING PAGE: *A wall of hard sell in light and color in 1926.* (PRECEDING PAGE, LEFT) *Enamel faces blew giant smoke rings into the air; neon fairies danced across rooftops. When Times Square prepared for its Millennium celebrations* (PRECEDING PAGE, RIGHT), *advertisers were paying up to $2 million a year in rent for a prominent billboard site.*

The Roxy Theater (LEFT AND TOP RIGHT), *an opulent display of gilded plasterwork, was billed as the "cathedral of the motion picture." Built in 1927 at a cost of $12 million, it could seat 6,000 patrons. The actress Gloria Swanson dramatically mourned its demolition in 1960* (BELOW LEFT). *It made way for an office block. The Apollo and Lyric theaters* (RIGHT *were turn-of-the-century arrivals on West 42nd Street, where a dozen theaters stood side by side on one block.*

decline, followed by the Depression's inroads into discretionary, leisure spending. Several sad decades followed. Times Square and, particularly, 42nd Street became bywords for sleaze. The flashing neon now peddled porn shows and X-rated movies. A remarkable feat of urban regeneration restored respect to the district in the 1990s though some mourned the loss of a center of vibrant vulgarity.

Billy Minsky's risqué burlesque shows featuring high-kicking chorus girls were modest fare compared with what was to come in the Times Square area. While the area waited for its regeneration, Haiku poets composed on the vacant marquees (ABOVE). Earlier, the movie houses competed to outshine each other with bright lights and comfort features. Warners' promised its 1926 patrons a "refrigerated washed-air cooling system."

SPORTS ARENAS
Fields of dreams

A BIG-LEAGUE SPORTS STADIUM – "an island in a sea of parking" – is not the most profitable tenant for prime real estate. Thus, generations of Manhattan fans have rooted for the Dodgers, the Jets, the Mets, and the Yankees, their baseball and football heroes, in the outer boroughs. Even the New York Knickerbockers, who gave rise to the notion that the city invented baseball by devising the rules of the modern game in the 1840s, played their games out of town, at New Jersey's Elysian Fields. Only the baseballing Giants were long-term performers on the island, at the Polo Grounds in Harlem, and they decamped to San Francisco in 1957.

The Polo Grounds set up for football (LEFT). The Giants and the Jets both played here, but the stadium was better known as the home of the baseballing Giants. It was the third Harlem stadium to bear the name; polo was actually played at the first one. This one, built of concrete and steel in 1912, made way for apartment blocks in the 1950s.

Forest Hills in Queens, home of the West Side Tennis Club, hosts the Davis Cup in 1959 (BELOW). Top-class tennis moved on to the USTA National Tennis Center at Flushing Meadows when this 13,000-capacity arena proved too small for the sport's burgeoning audience.

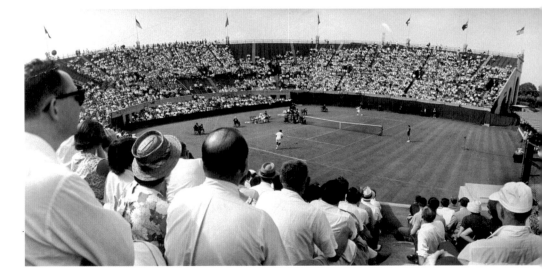

Shea Stadium, named for the attorney who brought National League baseball back to New York after the Giants and the Dodgers defected, is on the old World's Fair site in Flushing, Queens. It is notorious as the noisiest stadium in the major leagues, disturbed by aircraft descending into nearby La Guardia Airport. It is said that the site was chosen in the winter, when the flight paths are different.

The address 1700 Bedford Avenue is now that of an apartment complex, but it once identified Ebbets Field (ABOVE AND RIGHT), named for the owner of the Brooklyn Dodgers. The first televised ballgame was broadcast from here (1939); Jackie Robinson broke baseball's color barrier here (1947). The most compact of the city's major league ballparks, it was built for the 1913 season on cheap land – then known as Pigtown – that was well served by public transportation. Needing more seating and more parking than the small site could provide, the Dodgers moved to Los Angeles in 1957.

In 1923, the New York Yankees, who had previously shared the Polo Grounds with the Giants, moved to their new Yankee Stadium in the Bronx (LEFT). It was the largest ballpark in the country, needed for all the fans who wanted to see Babe Ruth; more than 70,000 of them, a baseball attendance record, filled "the house that Ruth built" for the opening game. The first triple-deck sports arena in the U.S., it was soon the best known, as successive star players emulated Ruth's triumphs. The Yankees threatened to leave town in the 1970s. The city spent $100 million upgrading the stadium to persuade them to stay.

MADISON SQUARE GARDEN CENTER

Circling the square

ARCHITECT
Charles Luckman
Associates

COMPLETED
1968

THERE HAVE BEEN FOUR different Madison Square Gardens where New Yorkers have been entertained and inspired, hoodwinked and scandalized: entertained by prizefights, horse shows, Barnum's circus, hockey, and basketball; inspired by FDR's endorsement of Al Smith, the city's favorite son, as Democratic Party candidate for the presidency; hoodwinked, briefly, by Mayor Jimmy Walker's rabble-rousing self-defense in the corruption scandal that was to end his stewardship of the city. And the scandal erupted when Stanford White, architect of the third and most distinguished of the sequence of Gardens, was murdered by a cuckolded husband in the roof garden of his Moorish-style masterpiece.

Least admired of the complexes to bear the name Madison Square Garden is the present one, which is on a different site from the others, between Seventh and Eighth Avenues at 31st Street. The disrespect is not so much to do with what it is, as motivated by nostalgic regard for the building it replaced – the much-loved, brutally demolished Penn Station (see p. 40), which had been designed by Stanford White's partner, Charles McKim.

Plans for a sports and entertainment complex based on a bowl-shaped arena had been on the drawing boards of the architects Charles Luckman Associates for a while as they waited for a suitable site. When Penn Station went underground, the bowl was built over it, together with Two Penn Plaza, an office block whose 29 stories exploited the newly available air rights.

The tower of Stanford White's Garden was, briefly, the second tallest structure in New York and boasted a fashionable cabaret room and the city's largest restaurant. The new Garden, purposefully squat, seats 20,000 spectators and there is a further auditorium on the site, the Felt Forum.

A circular lattice of steel tops out 13 stories in 1966 (ABOVE). Steel cables across the tension ring will support the roof so that there will be no pillars to interrupt spectators' viewing. The Garden was clad in glass and pre-cast concrete, as was the new office block that shared the site (LEFT). Stanford White's Madison Square Garden of 1890 (RIGHT), the second to bear the name, was the last to actually be at Madison Square.

MADISON   GARDEN N.Y. 392

LINCOLN CENTER FOR THE PERFORMING ARTS

Curtain up for the lively arts

PRINCIPAL ARCHITECTS
Philip Johnson, Wallace K.
Harrison, Max Abramovitz

COMPLETED
1962–68

SAN JUAN HILL, one of the city's more central and notorious slums, enjoyed a brief brush with fame when it was used as the location for the movie *West Side Story*. Then it was razed, to make way for politicking, music, and dancing of a different order. Critics had long sniped that New York was a wealth machine with no cultural soul. To make way for one, Robert Moses used his awesome planning powers to clear the area, displacing the community of Puerto Rican families.

In the 1960s, the Lincoln Center for the Performing Arts emerged on the site, bounded by Columbus and Amsterdam Avenues and 62nd and 66th Streets. Opera and symphony were to be top of the bill, then ballet, American repertory theater, and educational services from a library and museum devoted to the performing arts.

The most excitement was generated by the notion of a new home, finally, for the New York Metropolitan Opera. Its 80-year-old premises on Broadway were cramped and inadequate, originally designed, some said, so that its best lines of sight led to the boxes of wealthy benefactors rather than to action on the stage. A new opera house was to have been at the heart of the Rockefeller Center project in the 1930s; as it happened, John D. Rockefeller III was president of Lincoln Center when the move was finally made.

Moses insisted on a public space as the grand gateway to the complex; the image invoked and much discussed was that of the Piazza San Marco in Venice. The New York State Theater, the Met, and the Philharmonic Hall overlook it. Designed by different architects – Philip Johnson, Wallace K. Harrison, Max Abramovitz, among others – the Center's principal buildings failed to impress critics looking for architectural unity. But five million visitors a year enjoy the programs on offer.

Max Abramovitz inspects the 70-ft.-high tapered piers of his Philharmonic Hall (LEFT). Despite, the clutter of its construction (ABOVE RIGHT), the interior would have an unusual degree of spaciousness. Crystal chandeliers and swirling curves of the lobby in Wallace Harrison's Metropolitan Opera House (RIGHT) suggest the grandeur of classical opera houses. Dozens of designs were submitted before the Met's traditionalist requirements matched the architect's modernist ambitions.

The Philharmonic Hall ready for its opening concert in September, 1962. Music critics were not impressed: bass notes and pianissimo passages went unheard. Ten years later, the hall was renamed the Avery Fisher Hall, after the benefactor who paid $10 million toward its acoustical rebuilding.

The five marble arches of the
Met, the dominant frontage
on the plaza designed by
Philip Johnson. Inside, rich red
fabrics and gold leaf frame
Le Triomphe de la Musique,
a mural by Marc Chagall.
After all the false starts, the
estimated cost of the building
was $45 million.

Before the Lincoln Center, Carnegie Hall (under construction, ABOVE) had served the city's music lovers since 1891, as home of the New York Philharmonic Orchestra. The new center threatened its survival. Leopold Stokowski conducts in Carnegie Hall (RIGHT) in 1947, where he later performed a fanfare in repsonse to news that the hall had been saved from the wrecker's ball.
WILLIAM B. TUTHILL, 1891

The wrecker's ball struck the old Metropolitan Opera House (BELOW) on Broadway and 239th Street in 1967, when it was more than 80 years old. The architect had been J. C. Cady, who had never before designed a theater; the considerable part of the audience who could see only half the stage paid for his inexperience.

The streets of ships

MARINERS APPROACHING the Verrazano Narrows were at the nation's front door, and its service entrance. For New York was first and foremost a port city; all its prosperity stemmed from the waterfront. The immigrant population arrived here, as did cotton, meat, and grain, the country's wealth that shipped down the Hudson for dispersal and export, and the imports from Europe and all points south.

A two-mile stretch along the East River, South Street, was the earliest port on Manhattan, reached after just 17 miles of tacking across the Upper Bay. The east side of the island was the safer haven, protected from the prevailing winds and the winter ice floes that hurried down the Hudson River.

As steam engines and iron hulls overcame the natural hazards, the deeper water of the Hudson frontage came into use. The marshlands of West Street were filled to make anchorages there. Robert Fulton's pioneering North River Steamboat began a regular service to upstate Albany in 1810. Within a decade, there were regular sailings across the Atlantic to Liverpool – a scheduled service, not dependent on the weather or a full hold. At first, there was a reluctance to turn to steam power for the long voyage

Bowsprits and booms line South Street in 1883 (RIGHT); in the background, the proud new Brooklyn Bridge. Chandlers, sailmakers, and carvers of figureheads competed for business on the other side of the street, along with boarding houses, taverns, and brothels. The port was vital to the city, but not greatly admired. The New York

— the coal fuel took up so much cargo space; but once that reservation had been routed, crossing times came down from three weeks to ten days.

In time, a great horseshoe of piers covered the waterfront from 60th Street in the northwest, around the Battery to the shadows of the Brooklyn Bridge — the largest conglomeration of marine enterprise in the world, handling more traffic than the rest of the nation's ports put together. In the mid-19th century, half a million ships a year passed through the Narrows. Packet boats, sidewheel steamers, the graceful Clippers, warships, barges, tugs, ferries, and scows jostled for space and moorings.

Brooklyn took up some of the overflow, draining the tidal marshland of its shoreline north from Red Hook to build piers and warehouses. And, with a thought for the traffic farther north, toward Long Island Sound, the U.S. Army blasted rocks from the riverbed of Hell Gate, making the notorious channel less treacherous.

America's war effort kept the port of New York operating at full capacity through World War II. But then the rise of the road haulage industry — trucks could be more flexible in their routings than ships plying inland waterways — and the introduction of container ships for trans-oceanic freight began the decline. Vessels loading and unloading the truck-size steel containers required different berthing facilities, with dockside space for unloading and maneuvering that could not be accommodated on Manhattan's waterfront. The massive freighters steered to port, to newly built terminals in New Jersey.

Ferries were the only way across the Hudson in 1910 (LEFT). *Dredging maintained a 40-ft.-deep channel up to 59th Street for the great liners. Two sometime holders of the Blue Riband for the fastest Atlantic crossing are docked at Hudson piers in this 1939 photograph* (ABOVE): *the* Bremen, *second from bottom, and the* Normandie, *fifth, which crossed from Cherbourg at an average speed of 30.31 knots on her maiden voyage in 1935. Impounded here when World War II prevented a return to France, she caught fire and sank while being converted into a troopship.*

"Aviation
is established.
Nothing can stop it."

MAYOR FIORELLO LA GUARDIA

THE CITY'S AIRPORTS

Staking a claim to the sky

PAN AM TERMINAL
ARCHITECTS
Tibbetts-Abbett-McCarthy-
Stratton, with Ives, Turano
& Gardner

COMPLETED 1960

TWA TERMINAL
ARCHITECTS
Eero Saarinen & Associates
COMPLETED 1962

MAJOR LA GUARDIA, an aviation enthusiast, was determined that when the age of flying really took off, New York would remain the nation's principal port of entry. In 1941, the city bought 1,000 marshy acres along Jamaica Bay, centered on Idlewild golf course, and work began on its biggest-ever construction project, an international airport. As ambitions grew, the perimeter fence came to enclose a further 4,000 acres. The largest land reclamation project in the country's history required almost 70 million cubic yards of sand to level the site and blot the wetlands.

Idlewild became fully operational in July, 1948. The never-ending construction program produced buildings that were functional rather than exciting, speedily erected as every forecast of likely air traffic was overwhelmed by actuality.

Two of America's leading flag-carriers, Pan Am and TWA, did, however, choose to make their terminals futuristic architectural statements. And at the Admiral's Club in the American Airlines building, first-class passengers were illuminated through the world's largest stained glass window, a 317-ft. curve, 22 ft. high.

But the city's best-loved airport building remains the Marine Air Terminal at La Guardia (Delano & Aldrich, 1939), whose Art Deco interior has Landmark preservation status. Once the departure point for flying boat services, the terminal later came to serve the

more mundane shuttles within the Bos-Wash megalopolis.

La Guardia Airport itself was an earlier initiative of the city's forward-thinking mayor. On a TWA flight from Chicago, he was enraged when the plane landed at Newark, New Jersey, and insisted on being delivered to his city, as the ticket promised. The plane flew on to Floyd Bennett Field, alongside Flatbush Avenue in Brooklyn.

The mayor's campaign to develop Floyd Bennett foundered, and a site for New York Municipal Airport was chosen in Queens, to take advantage of the new Queens–Midtown Tunnel to Manhattan. The airport opened in December 1939. Within a few days it had been renamed Fiorello La Guardia Airport. It remains the city's hub for domestic flights.

The mayor's ambition for the city's place in commercial aviation certainly came to pass. Fifty years later, three-fourths of trans-oceanic flights were across the Atlantic, and half those were to and from New York, to John F. Kennedy, as Idlewild had become, and Newark.

The Pan Am terminal (PRECEDING PAGE AND LEFT). *From a 100,000-sq-ft. oval building, a four-acre steel and concrete umbrella is cantilevered out to cover parked aircraft. Bronze zodiac figures sculpted by Milton Hebald decorate the windshield protecting the forecourt. Critics considered this a "trite" idea, not befitting a bold building. Within a decade, the airline needed a facility seven times the size; 20 years after that, it was out of business.*

The severely formal Marine Air
Terminal at La Guardia was built to
serve a more gracious era of air travel,
when Pan Am Clipper flying boats
(RIGHT, in 1940), cruised down the
Atlantic coast to Rio. The circular
waiting area carries a mural, Flight,
by James Brooks, later painted over,
then restored. A frieze of flying fish
commemorates the Clipper days.

For TWA, Eero Saarinen aimed to express "movement and transition." He designed "a big bird," the roof shaped like spread wings. There are curvilinear forms everywhere, shaping display boards, check-in desks, and stairways. Passengers walk to the departure gates along "jetways," disorientating tubular corridors; they were to have been motorized, but the airline's financial difficulties caused budget cuts. TWA was ambivalent about the award of landmark status to the building, on the grounds that it might prevent them replacing obsolete spaces and equipment.

ROBERT MOSES
Power over the people

WHEN FEDERAL FUNDS FROM President Roosevelt's New Deal became available for the city's public projects, New York had a big spender ready and eager to use them. Robert Moses, modestly titled Parks Commissioner, now had the money to press on with his vision for transforming the city, its suburbs, and its hinterland. And as the coins collected from the tolls on his Triborough Bridge were added to the stash, the dotted lines on his planning map quickly became realities of steel, concrete, and asphalt.

Never elected to office, never accountable to voters, Moses exercised power through a dozen state and city titles that he collected between 1924 and 1968. Bankers and bondholders, politicians, contractors, and labor union leaders (in the late 1930s, 80,000 people were employed on his projects) were sucked into a maelstrom of activity, awed by his personality, the wealth at his disposal, and the favors he could dispense and withhold. During his tenure, Moses opened up 10,000 acres of parks on Long Island, and the means for city-dwellers to reach them. He built 13 vehicular spans and more miles of superhighway – more than 400 – than Los Angeles. He tore out the rusting railroad tracks that ringed Manhattan to landscape riverside drives. The city gained 250 playgrounds and 11 municipal swimming pools.

But there was a human cost to this progress. A critic said of Moses, "he loves the public, but he hates people." The public he pleased was white, middle-class, car-owning; the people who paid the price were African-Americans and Puerto Ricans. Expressways plowed through neighborhoods where mellow integration had been achieved. As the better quality public-private housing projects touted as replacement homes were rarely available to these minorities, they were forced into bleak blocks or back into ghettoes. Only one of Moses's playgrounds was built in Harlem; black children still took their summer coolings from the fire hydrants on their streets.

Robert Moses never learned to drive, but he truly embraced the age of the automobile; subway development was put on hold during his tenure. And he was the first city planner to experience the phenomenon that would dog all future urbanization: the more roads that are built, the more automobiles there will be to fill them. Moses's response was to bulldoze another neighborhood for another thruway. It was not until the residents of Greenwich Village realized that their treasured community was threatened in this way that the first articulate alarm was raised. Moses was forced to reconsider, and his power began to decline.

An unexpected success at the toll booths, a new kind of problem for traffic cops, and a sidewalk show for residents of Queens, the Triborough Bridge gives an early indication (ABOVE) of its potential for changing urban economics and weekend habits. More than half a century later, the Verrazano Narrows Bridge (RIGHT) is put to a use Robert Moses never imagined — as the first stage of the New York City Marathon. The runners' route takes in all five boroughs.

EXPRESSWAYS

Fast tracking traffic

CARVING ROADS THROUGH social trouble spots was a much-practiced 19th-century answer to the fear of urban unrest. New Oxford Street in London drove through the "rookery" of St. Giles, the city's most notorious, gin-soaked slum, dispersing its unruly residents. Emperor Napoleon III authorized the town planner Haussmann to reconfigure Paris around broad spokes of avenues that the mobs would not be able to barricade. In New York, the combustible community of Five Points was buried under the streets meeting at Foley Square, north of City Hall.

London and Paris have hardly built a major downtown highway since. But a century later, Robert Moses returned to the practice. Pursuing his ambition to re-create New York for the age of the automobile, he diplaced more than 300,000 people, a clumsy response to another of his responsibilities – slum clearance. The Cross-Bronx Expressway alone displaced 40,000 people, on brutally short notice; the gain was Bronx/Queens access to New Jersey, upper New York State, and the New England resorts.

Automobile drivers, truckers, and bus operators were eased into the city, and given routes around it. In the 1940s, Moses had even invoked a Nazi initiative to press for his projects: New York should have defense highways, in the manner of Hitler's autobahn network. (And, indeed, that line of thinking would become an argument for the interstate highways system.)

In the early 1950s, his planning maps were overlaid with ribbons indicating six new expressways. All of them took shape as the torrents of asphalt and concrete smothered anything in their path. The rivers that separated the boroughs were no longer of consequence to traffic flow. The promise at the eastern end of the Queens Midtown Tunnel was the Long Island Expressway, soon to be overwhelmed by commuters as urban sprawl spread along its length.

Robert Moses built his headquarters under the tollbooths of the Triborough Bridge, a short drop from the income he totally controlled (LEFT). But he did spend generously on community projects such as the landscaping and stadium seen here. The columns in the top-left of the photograph support the Hell Gate railroad bridge.

Not even Robert Moses could get right to the waterfront for this 1953 section of the East Side Highway, part of the ring road that was intended to outline Manhattan. Rubble for earlier construction came from blitzed London – carried as ballast on ships that had ferried World War II supplies to Europe (OVERLEAF).

Outside Moses's domain, but nevertheless crucial to his plans, the New Jersey Turnpike heads toward his city in 1951. It would link with the Staten Island Expressway, the Verrazano Narrows Bridge, the city's airports, and New England.

PARKWAYS

A new look for highways

A CENTURY AGO, THE BRONX RIVER, meandering down from Westchester County through a scenic valley, had become a malodorous, rubbish-strewn eyesore. There could be little complaint, then, if the wooded hillsides were underlined with concrete. In 1923, the highway, 15 miles built at a cost of $1 million a mile, opened as a controlled-access road, without intersections or stoplights, a gently curving, tree-lined, landscaped route into the city for the affluent commuters of Scarsdale and White Plains.

It was a "parkway," the Bronx River Parkway. Both the word and the idea are particular to New York. No other

The Merritt Parkway roughly parallels the Connecticut coast-line of Long Island Sound, leading out to waterfront state parks, opening up New England. Parkways were for cars only, adapting to the topography rather than leveling it with expressway rigidity. They created a travel environment suiting the notion that driving was a pleasure in itself. Low bridges ensured that there would be no trucks to spoil the effect.

American metropolis has so carefully fitted so many miles of access and exit so homogeneously into the landscape. The concept perfectly suited the urban dreams of Robert Moses, and soon there were many more parkways, reaching north, and east into Long Island: the Hutchinson River Parkway, the Saw Mill River, the Cross Island, the Belt, the Grand Central, and more.

Within the city limits alone there are 100 miles of parkways that Moses built, most dramatically Manhattan's Henry Hudson Parkway. Here he rooted out the rusting tracks of the old New York Central Railroad and the detritus of an industrial waterfront to give motorists, his favored species among New Yorkers, majestic views across the river to the Palisades of New Jersey, and landscaped recreational facilities if they cared to stop.

NEW YORK WORLD'S FAIR 1939

Promise of the future on the eve of war

NEW YORK'S 1939 WORLD'S FAIR rose from the ashes of incinerated garbage and, bravely, damped down the embers of the Depression. The 1,200-acre site in northern Queens was the Corona Dump, beside Flushing Bay, "a malodorous eyesore" whose name would be quietly sanitized in favor of the more pastoral-sounding Flushing Meadow. The fair's theme was "Building the World of Tomorrow," and in the vision of Parks Commissioner Robert Moses, that was a world of automobiles. The corporate pavilions of carmakers Chrysler, Ford, and General Motors eagerly promoted the notion.

GM's Futurama exhibit was the most ambitious, a 36,000-sq. ft. model of the United States, as it would be 20 years on if the auto industry had its way. It showed skyscraper cities served by 14-lane highways buzzing with the private vehicles of commuters from single-family homes in the suburbs. There was no place in this society for buses, subways, or railroads. And no sign of a ghetto. For this dream, New York as it presently was would need to be razed and rebuilt.

At the heart of the two-square-mile fairground, approached along the Avenue of Patriots or the Avenue of Pioneers, two dramatic structural shapes made futuristic statements: the Trylon, a tapering, three-sided shaft 610 ft. tall, gave entry to the Perisphere, a 180-ft. diameter globe inside which revolving platforms, "magic carpets," transported visitors around Democracity, an ideal community for 1,000,000 comfortable citizens.

But there was a roadblock on the route to the world of tomorrow – World War II was already overwhelming Europe. When the fair reopened for the 1940 season, the Czech and Polish pavilions had closed, the Soviet exhibit was demolished in outrage at the signing of the Stalin-Hitler non-aggression pact, and fallen France's Tricolor flew at half mast.

The fair wound down in an atmosphere of increasing gloom. Steel from the dismantled buildings was put aside for the war effort. The return to bondholders was 39 cents on the dollar. The lasting legacy was more miles of highway, the roads that Robert Moses built to smooth the journeys of 40 million fair visitors — half the expected number: the Whitestone Expressway and the Bronx-Whitestone Bridge, the Grand Central and Cross Island parkways. Ironically, with a bridge toll and a 50 cent parking fee, a family of four from almost anywhere in the five boroughs spent less to get there if they traveled by subway.

The Perisphere, under construction (RIGHT), was the fair's statement building. Fountains of water hid the mirror-encased columns that would support it. At night, projected light made the globe appear to revolve.

(OVERLEAF) Visitors queue for the Perisphere show, a six-minute vision of life in Democracity, where 250,000 people work downtown, each, apparently, supporting a family of four who live in suburban houses and garden apartments.

The photographic record of the fair appears most elegantly in the work of Alfred Eisenstadt, a refugee from Nazi Germany who joined Life magazine, the pioneer of modern photojournalism. The fair was the last hurrah for institutional Art Décor, and Eisenstadt dwelt on the swooping shapes and fantasy decoration.

(OVERLEAF) General Motors encased its Futurama exhibit in streamlined Modernism. Inside, visitors in moving "soundchairs" circled around an America of the 1960s, where cars hurtled along highways at 100 mph. The railroads fought back, from a building decorated with classical reliefs, with a pageant that told their story.

Reprising the future

Robert Moses bullied his way to the helm of the 1964 World's Fair, but by now he had doubters and detractors all the way to the top of the political pyramid. The price he paid for control of the fair was the loss of the several city appointments that were his power base, his unaccountable fiefdoms.

Once in command, he ousted the enthusiastic instigator of the project, the lawyer Robert Kopple. Then he defied and insulted the Bureau of International Expositions ("three people living obscurely in a dumpy apartment in Paris"), who responded by urging other member nations not to participate. It was Moses at his most authoritarian, and yet his heart seemed not to be in the project. The hindsight view is that his real interest was in maximizing income from the fair, to fund the creation on the site – again, it was Flushing Meadow – of the grandest of all his parks. Perhaps the one that would bear his name for all time? Exhibitors paid ten times the rentals of the 1939 fair; and Moses tried to block concessionary entrance rates for schoolchildren.

At a time when American public architecture badly needed the budget for a visionary jolt out of Modernist complacency, Moses spent as little as he could on the theme buildings. The overall result was a disappointing hodgepodge. The hard sell of a trade fair overwhelmed the theme of "Peace through Understanding." Walt Disney got involved, begging the question "was Flushing Meadow to be the next Disneyland?" It wasn't – northern seaboard weather was too variable for Mickey Mouse.

IBM's "egg" takes shape (BELOW). *The exhibit it would contain had the Fair's most significant message for the future: computers will change everything.*

Visitors to Futurama, the General Motors pavilion, approached a 10-story -high aluminum façade angled out over a plaza (ABOVE). Its inspiration was the huge tail fins of cars of the time – "good advertising but ridiculous architecture."

(OVERLEAF) The orbits of NASA satellites proudly circled the Unisphere – the theme building. The land masses were formed from stainless steel sheeting weighing, with the cage, 900,000 lbs. To prove the design, computers did what the engineers reckoned were 10 years' worth of calculations. "A trite cartoon in iron," one critic called it, but it is still there. Philip Johnson and Richard Foster designed the New York State Pavilion in the background: concrete towers supporting canopies of colored plastic.

General Motors was back. This time the roads to carry its products traversed the Sahara, carved through the jungles of South America, and skated across Antarctica – routes without purpose or passengers. "Weary and wistful," the commentators thought.

There were more realistic visions. In one of the fair's more admired structures – a steel-framed ovoid standing tall on steel "trees," designed by Eero Saarinen with Charles Eames interiors – IBM indicated the potential of the computer in everyday lives. AT&T demonstrated a "picturephone" that would, for better or worse, come to market. And Ford introduced the Mustang, which soon became America's all-time favorite car.

However, for the second time, a New York World's Fair would be overshadowed by outside events. Newly confident civil rights activists threatened disruption, and the conflict in Vietnam was gathering momentum. The site did indeed become a park: Flushing Meadows/Corona Park, a large, welcome, though undistinguished breathing space for the city. A few of the fair's structures were left standing – eccentric outcrops that can still be seen on the drive into Manhattan from JFK Airport.

"Nobody
departs,until it
closes, From the
Promised Land of
Mr Moses."

OGDEN NASH, poet

This was a dismal section of the Bronx (ABOVE) until the Metropolitan Life Insurance Company built the huge residential complex of Parkchester, a suburb in its own right. MetLife provided shopping, parking, and land-scaping — but no churches or schools. The photographer Alfred Eisenstadt noticed "Mary Poppins" decorating the corner of one block (RIGHT).
RICHMOND H. SHREVE, 1942

HOUSING PROJECTS
Apartments for all

I F THE ISLAND OF MANHATTAN HAD filled at the density of the most miserable Lower East Side ghettoes, it would have had eight million residents. The social stain of tenement overcrowding was still on the minds of reformers half a century after the 1880s, and the issue of housing the less well-off remained a pressing one. In Harlem in the late 1930s, rents for accommodation officially deemed unfit for human habitation could take well over half a family's income; "hot beds" served three shifts of sleepers a day.

Fiorello La Guardia, "the People's Mayor," took the problem seriously. Encouraged by "municipal socialists," his New York City Housing Authority became the first agency in the country to challenge the monopoly of private real estate interests in the housing market, attracting federal funds, state backing, and bond support from among Robert Moses's contacts.

At a dedication ceremony in 1935, Eleanor Roosevelt sat alongside La Guardia as First Houses, the nation's first public housing project, made some amends for the neglect of the Lower East Side.

The Astor family had sold the city the land for it at a knock-down price. The Rockefellers made a similar gesture in Harlem, enabling the financial feasibility of Harlem River Houses where, in 1937, the new apartments could be rented for around $25 a month. The simplistic, back-of-the-envelope calculation for the mayor's planners was, can we build here to rent at $10 a room? At Red Hook Houses in Brooklyn, the promise for the 1939 opening was 2,560 apartments at a room-rate of $6 a month.

The City Housing Authority sought to observe social boundaries, to place people in neighborhoods among their own kind. Robert Moses's dealings led to a more callous interpretation of the notion, allowing developers to overtly restrict leases to whites during and immediately after World War II. Civil rights groups were still campaigning against such policies in the 1960s.

But the high-rise apartment blocks went on rising, publicly and privately funded. For Peter Cooper Village at First Avenue and 20th Street, 500 buildings were demolished in 1945 to make way for 2,500 apartments. Parkchester set the buildings to contain 12,000 units over 130 acres, gracing them with landscaped gardens, parking for 3,000 cars, and Macy's first store outside Manhattan. At Stuyvesant Town, 35

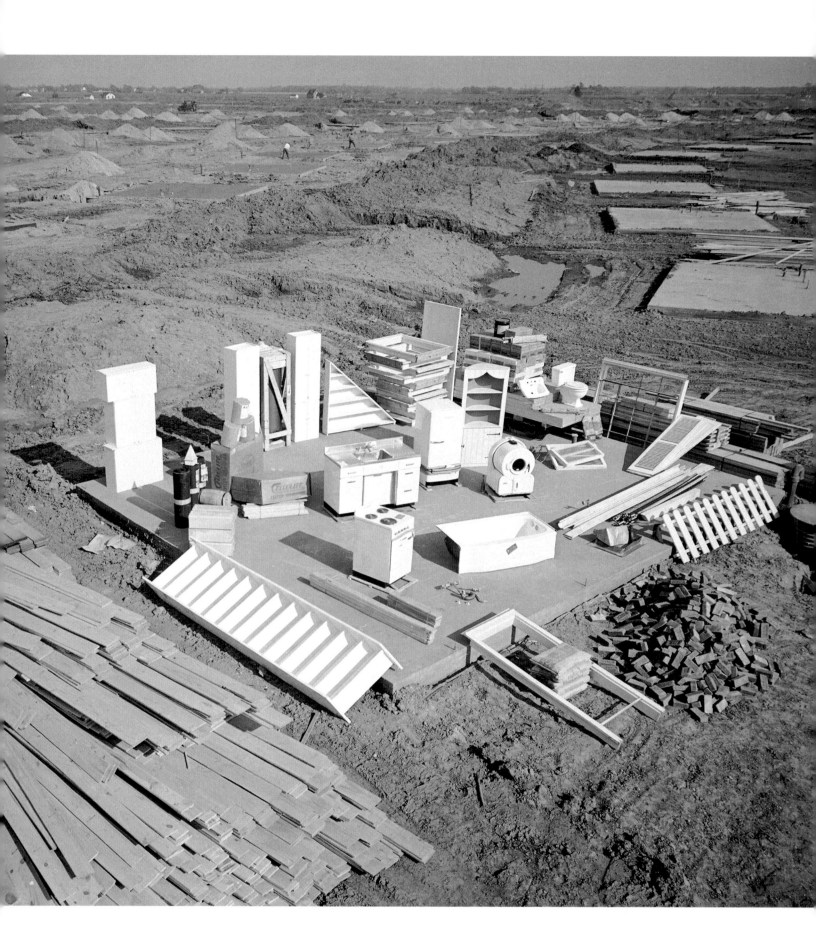

The concrete slab foundation (ABOVE) with its radiant-heating coil is in place; sidings, cooking range, refrigerator, stand ready for the "assembly line" construction of a Levittown house, one of 17,000 identical structures on a 4,000-acre Long Island potato field. These were homes for heroes, veterans returning from World War II. Helped by G.I. mortgage assistance, they would pay $8,000 for a two-bedroom, one bathroom, fully equipped house (RIGHT), though the attic could be developed at the owner's discretion. The wage-earner, it was thought, would commute the 30 miles into Manhattan, or work at one of the defense industry contractors that were expected to dominate the Long Island economy during the Cold War.

(OVERLEAF) *Snowflakes soften Peter Cooper Village and Stuyvesant Town, downtown on First Avenue. Many thought its bleak blocks a war-weary failure to rethink inner-city living; many tenants were delighted to find a "first real home" – for $75 a month.*
IRWIN CLAVAN AND GILMORE CLARKE, 1947

brick blocks of 13 and 14 stories contained almost 9,000 apartments, all of them rented when occupancy commenced in 1947.

Like all the world's major cities, New York continues to face the problem of providing enough low-income housing. But it has done better than most, particularly with municipally sponsored projects in Brooklyn and the Bronx.

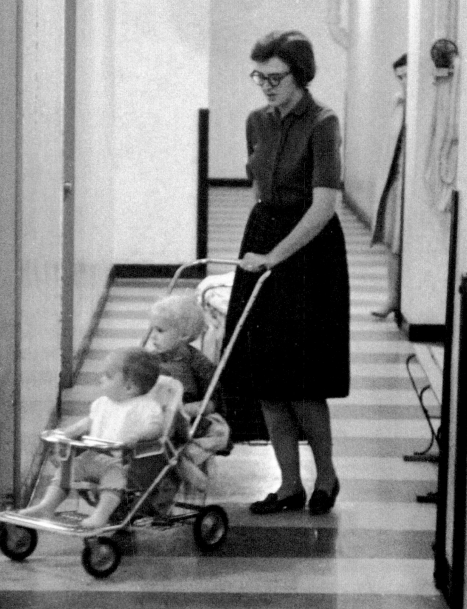

Young families quickly filled the 100,000 apartments of Lefrak City, a private-sector development in Rego Park, Queens. When the complex was being built in the 1960s, billboards overlooking stalled commuter traffic on the Long Island Expressway made the point, "If you lived here, you would be home by now."
JACK BROWN, 1967

Filling the sky with logos

AFTER THE UGLY DISTRACTIONS of the Depression and World War II, New York returned to the relentless pursuit of its primary ambition, to make money. And as the 1950s progressed, new reasons arose for adventurous entrepreneurs to settle there. The city was now quite clearly the nation's powerhouse for the age of television; which meant that anyone with a consumer product to sell on air had to have a presence alongside the Madison Avenue advertising agencies. As the headquarters of the United Nations, Manhattan came to be perceived as the "executive city" for businesses with global ambitions. And the new "world economy," informed by new generations of communications systems, propelled Wall Street to international status, requiring vast recruitment in the financial sector.

The builders responded. In 1950, they created 4 million sq. ft. of office space; in 1960, 6 million sq. ft.; almost 14 million in 1970. Older buildings were razed to make way for taller ones; 40 stories became the median height.

But what was the architectural style to be? Over on the East River, Le Corbusier's statement was International Style Modernist: the United Nations Secretariat building he inspired faced the city with a sheer wall of glass. On Park Avenue, the Lever House balanced one mostly glass block on another. Then, across the street, Mies van der Rohe and Philip Johnson spent more money per sq. ft. than had ever been spent before, on the Seagram Building, all bronzed glass punctuated by bronze I-beams.

Lever, Seagram, PanAm – the skyline filled with a new generation of corporate statements, emblems of influence and power. For the community, the danger was that these big, bullying blocks sapped humanity from the streets. To an extent, new planning laws found an answer. Instead of the "wedding cake" setback style of earlier skyscrapers, these straight-sided monsters brought the "plaza bonus." They could rise, sheer, but their size was limited by how much space at ground level was given over to plazas, malls, arcades, and terraces open to the public. In the 1960s, 1 million sq. ft. of breathing space was provided for the congested city in this way. For property developers, the upside was that for every dollar's worth of plaza, they could add $48 of rentable space. The average height of new buildings went up by 10 floors.

By its very nature – minimalist, undecorated – International Style Modernism had to become monotonous. The line under it was drawn at the World Trade Center, which had little going for it architecturally except its height. The remoteness from the community such towers suggested led to visions of "social skyscrapers," mixed-use buildings playing some part in everyday life. The white, aluminum-clad Citicorp Center on Lexington Avenue (1977) makes a brave attempt to be sociable, even housing a church in its plaza.

What next? Postmodern, Romantic Modern, Postmodern Classical – Philip Johnson placed a "Chippendale" pediment on top of his AT&T Building. Or will it be Polychromatic Futuristic, Modern Expressionism? The search for style continues.

The sparkling aluminum-clad tower of the Citicorp Center rests on 130-ft.-high columns, allowing New York street life to continue underneath.

Cantankerous, egocentric, messianic in his promotion of the International Style, Le Corbusier (RIGHT) sketched a vision for the U.N. headquarters that was broadly followed. Too difficult to work with, he was removed from the project, claimed it as his own, and sniped at its fulfilment from his base in Paris.

Vermont marble facing climbs the northern wall of the Secretariat Building (LEFT). The 287-ft.-wide east and west sides introduced the use of glass curtain-walling – more than 10,000 sheets of blue-green heat-absorbing glass that became a landmark for their reflections of the city around them.

SLOW
CROSSOVER →

KEEP
RIGHT

UNITED NATIONS HEADQUARTERS

The world convenes on First Avenue

DIRECTOR OF PLANNING
Wallace K. Harrison

COMPLETED
1952

IT WAS A CLOSE-RUN THING: the United Nations almost went to Philadelphia. In December 1946, just days before the secretary general's deadline for a decision, and with an attractive bid from the City of Brotherly Love in place, the Rockefeller brothers, Nelson and David, identified a suitable site in Manhattan, a family profit center, and persuaded their father to pay for it. Just hours before the deadline, the owner accepted their offer.

The site was an unpromising four-block tract on the East Side, 18 acres of decaying slaughterhouses and meat-packing plants known politely as Turtle Bay and colloquially as Blood Alley. The price was $8.5 million. After the Rockefellers' speedy footwork, it was Robert Moses' turn. Exercising his awesome planning powers, manipulating his contacts in Albany and City Hall, he quickly completed the conveyancing of city land and waterfront rights, and authorized street clearances. New York, still resentful that it was not the nation's capital, could now imagine itself as capital of the world.

A team of international architects was appointed, under the leadership of Wallace K. Harrison, a Rockefeller nominee, but it was the eccentric Swiss-born visionary Le Corbusier who would be perceived as the inspiration. Certainly, he thought so. For this city within a city – its administrative relationship to New York would be similar to that of the Vatican City's to Rome – he planned an abstract composition of buildings, high and low, linear and curved.

The ground-breaking ceremony for the Secretariat building took place in September 1948. It grew to 544 ft., 39 stories, an unadorned block whose sheer glass sides would be regularly replicated in New York's post-war skyscraper boom. Almost simultaneously, excavation began for the least visible unit in the complex, the five-story Conference Building, housing, most

A slab wall of English Portland Stone dramatizes the concave curve of the General Assembly building's roofline (ABOVE). The ramp leads to the delegates' entrance. Vertical stripes of marble and translucent glass surround the visitors' doors.

A tapestry version of Picasso's Guernica reminds delegates entering the Security Council of their mission to preserve the peace (RIGHT).

A self-sufficient, self-policing international territory, the U.N. complex (FAR RIGHT) has street and waterfront rights along the East River from 42nd to 48th streets. Architecturally, it was Le Corbusier's sermon to the city around it; he considered New York a "catastrophe."

Wallace K. Harrison (ABOVE) led the team of architects chosen from the U.N.'s founder nations. He was associated with the Rockefellers' most ambitious projects, such as Rockefeller Center and Lincoln Center, with the theme buildings of the 1939 World's Fair, and La Guardia Airport. On the U.N. project, much of his energy went to countering Le Corbusier's intemperate attacks on the team's enactment of his vision.

Marbled glass filters the northern light flooding the 75-ft.-high General Assembly lobby (ABOVE RIGHT). The lowest of the three cantilevered balconies is reached from a ramp supported by parabolic arches. The hall itself seats 850 delegates in mildly terraced rows, under a huge dome. That was an afterthought; U.S. congressmen whose support for funding was needed insisted on it. They could not imagine a political forum without one.

importantly, the Security Council, behind a 400-ft. frontage overlooking the East River. Then a blank wall arose on the First Avenue side of the site, topped, surprisingly, by a bold, dipping curve, an hourglass shape, a saddle back. With the General Assembly building in place, observers from the city side could see the outlines Le Corbusier had in mind.

As civil servants from around the world moved in, the New York economy took a welcome lift. Multinational corporations now had to consider whether their headquarters should be alongside this center of global influence. And empty offices at Rockefeller Center, just five blocks away, began to fill. The family's $8.5 million donation looked like money well spent.

The Security Council room, one of three main chambers in the Conference Building. Three Scandinavian architects designed the interiors; in this case, the architect of Oslo's town hall. Walls, upholstery, and drapes are in royal blue fabrics decorated with gold.

SEAGRAM BUILDING

A masterpiece on Park Avenue

ARCHITECTS
Ludwig Mies van der Rohe
with Philip Johnson

COMPLETED
1958

SAMUEL BRONFMAN, PRESIDENT of the Seagram distilling company, was overruled by his daughter in the choice of architect for a corporate headquarters. He had chosen from the team that had just built the Lever House, across Park Avenue from the Seagram site, a glass-sided echo of Le Corbusier's U.N. Secretariat building. Phyllis Bronfman Lambert persuaded her father that the design was mediocre. What's more, she said, this is a time of great architects. Let's hire one.

She selected the world-renowned Mies van der Rohe, a professor at the Illinois Institute of Technology in Chicago, a disciple of Le Corbusier's who had never worked in New York. In turn, Mies chose as his partner, Philip Johnson, the well-connected architect who was his most vocal advocate in the city. Between them, they spent more money per square foot than had ever before been lavished on a building: more than $40 million including the cost of the land.

On the building's completion in 1958, the patron, the architectural establishment, critics, and New Yorkers in general all agreed that it was money well spent. The consensus was that the Seagram Building was New York's most successful post-war building – "a muted masterpiece." Yes, it was another slab-sided monster, but it occupied less than half its plot, set back 90 ft. from the street in a half-acre plaza where fountains played. The simple surfaces exuded quality: bronzed I-beams accentuated the verticals, outlining custom-tinted amber glass. Expensive attention to detail showed in every facet, inside and out.

It looked easy and was much copied; and if the Seagram Building did a disservice to New York architecture, it was in the careless and cut-price replication it inspired. Glass-walling, bleak and bland, became the cliché that halted further innovation.

To one observer, the Seagram Building's facings were "a frank and bold mask." Another thought they diminished the humanity of people inside, making them look like "flies in amber." Given the trade of its owners, it was to some, inevitably, "the gin palace."

Ludwig Mies van der Rohe headed the influential Bauhaus school of art and architecture in Berlin until the Nazis closed it in 1933. A pioneer of the International Style, he gave his name to the term Miesian Aesthetic: in essence, "less is more."

*At 38 stories and 500 ft.,
the Seagram Building was not
competing to be tallest. But
the extravagant setback from
the street allows passers-by
on Park Avenue to appreciate
the whole edifice in a glance.
The tax authorities were less
admiring of the open space: it
denied them income from the
rentable office accommodation
that might have been there.*

No expense was spared inside either. Modern classics designed by Mies van der Rohe furnish the Seagram reception area. The canopy (LEFT) covers the entrance to a 24-ft.-high lobby with travertine floors and walls and a glass ceiling. The building contains a notable restaurant, the Four Seasons, decorated by Philip Johnson at a cost of $4 million. It is hung with works of art by, among others, Picasso, Joan Miró, and Jackson Pollock.

A helicopter service brought Pan Am passengers from JFK to the heart of the city – until a fatal crash on the rooftop ended the operation in 1977.

PAN AM BUILDING

The tower that spoiled the view

ARCHITECTS
Emery Roth & Sons,
Walter Gropius,
Pietro Belluschi

COMPLETED
1963

GRAND CENTRAL IS CONSIDERED to be the city's center of gravity. When its railroad-operating owners sought to exploit the air rights above it in the 1950s, they were warned, whatever is built here will be the city's most important structure. What resulted is, by common consent, New York's least-liked building.

Nearing the top: steel framing for the 59th story goes into place (ABOVE).

The bulk of the building is to the north of the station, but it was accused of "appropriating the Grand Central façade as if it were its own" (RIGHT).

It was to be called Grand Central City. Then Pan Am World Airways took options on enough of its space – at a total of 2.4 million sq. ft., more than any other office building in the world at the time – to be allowed to emblazon their name on the sides. The Pan Am Building, a flattened octagon framed in pre-cast concrete, sat astride Park Avenue. At a time when slim metal columns and curtains of glass were lightening the skyline – most successfully in the Seagram Building, which it overlooked – here was a return to the stone age. What's more, it was a visual dead stop to Park Avenue, the city's finest boulevard.

Commercially, the building got off to a flying start: 90 percent of its space was leased by opening day. And the Grand Central commuters who found employment there appreciated its convenience: four elevators from the station's Grand Concourse took them to the Pan Am lobby, housing cafes, restaurants, and convenience stores, then 60 elevators fed work stations on 50 floors.

Pan Am World Airways crashed out of business in 1992. The signs high on the walls now say "Met Life," for the Metropolitan Life Insurance Company.

TRUMP TOWER

Building on the name

ARCHITECTS
Der Scutt; Swanke Hayden
Connell

COMPLETED
1983

*Donald Trump's high profile
in New York led to speculation
that he would be a candidate
for the U.S. presidency. His
vision statement was, "You can
see a long way from the top of
the Trump Tower."*

*Welcome to conspicuous
consumption Trump-style, where
window shopping begins the
moment customers step on the
escalators rising through the six-
story marble atrium. Trees and
shrubs soften the staggered
stepbacks of the bronzed glass
exterior. Trump bought the
air rights (for $5 million,
according to realtor gossip)
of the low building across
the street to permit extra
height for his tower.*

DYNASTIES HAVE INFLUENCED the shaping of New York. After the Astors, the Vanderbilts, and the Rockefellers came families like the Zeckendorfs, father and son; the Tishmans, father, sons, son-in-law. And Fred Trump, a modest developer of outer suburbs, whose son, Donald, came to symbolize all that was brazen and bruising about success in the city.

Fred Trump put the family name on a Coney Island housing complex, Trump Village. Donald took eponymity to a new level: the Trump Building, a revamping and renaming of the Bank of the Manhattan Company building, for a few days in the 1920s, the world's tallest; Trump Place, in what was going to be called Trump City; Trump World Tower, a 900-ft.-high apartment block at the U.N. Plaza; Trump Plaza on Third Avenue; Trump International Hotel and Tower where, with the help of the eminent architect Philip Johnson, he peeled the skin off an ailing building that dominated Columbus Circle and restored it; the Trump Shuttle, a foray into the airline business. And then the showpiece statement, Trump Tower, a monumental, gleaming example of "late modernism" on Fifth Avenue at 56th Street.

From the day liveried attendants opened its doors for the first time, in 1983, Trump Tower has been a tourist attraction. Among six levels of boutique stores, a grand piano vies for aural attention with a waterfall. Above this commercial display are 20 floors of offices and 40 floors of apartments, one of which, with a 360-degree view over the city, was once put on the market with a $62 million asking price.

LEVER HOUSE ON PARK AVENUE, A RECTANGULAR SLAB STANDING ON ANOTHER THAT CONTAINS AN OPEN COURTYARD. THIS WAS THE FIRST GLASS-WALLED COMMERCIAL BLOCK TO BE COMPLETED IN NEW YORK.
Gordon Bunshaft, 1952

885 THIRD AVENUE, KNOWN TO ALL NEW YORKERS AS THE LIPSTICK BUILDING – FOR ITS ELLIPTICAL SHAPE AND STRIATIONS OF PINK AND BROWN.
John Burgee, Philip Johnson, 1986

THE ANGLED SURFACE ROOFING THE CITICORP CENTER ON LEXINGTON AVENUE WAS TO HAVE BEEN A SOLAR COLLECTOR – AN UNFULFILLED EFFORT TO BE SOCIALLY RESPONSIBLE.
Hugh Stubbins & Associates, 1978

Now the Sony Building, but built for AT&T, this post-Modernist statement appeared on Madison Avenue in 1984. In an era of glass walling, Philip Johnson returned to masonry cladding, and topped the building with a flourish – a "Chippendale" pediment.

WORLD TRADE CENTER

Downtown's doomed symbol

ARCHITECTS
Minoru Yamasaki & Associates,
Emery Roth & Sons

COMPLETED
1973

*The unforgettable symbols
of downtown's rejuvenation
nearing completion in 1971
(ABOVE). Excavating the site
provided 23 acres of landfill
for Battery Park City nearby
on the Hudson.*

*"Gothic lancets" taper into
strong faces that will be locked
together at the corners (RIGHT).
The Trade Center was
completed ahead of schedule
but, at $800 million, it cost
twice the first budget estimates.*

IT SEEMED TO THE BUILDERS of the Twin Towers of the World Trade Center that the biggest threat to the world's tallest structures would be winds blustering off the Hudson and the Upper Bay. Their answer was a return to the principles of an earlier architectural age: strength on the outside, the rigidity of load-bearing walls. These would not be goliaths in glass like most skyscrapers of the 1960s.

The two monoliths rose to their full 1,250-ft. height as hollow tubes, formed by a mesh of aluminum-faced steel – columns and cross-beams in a lattice punctuated by setback windows just 22 in. wide.

Inside, only the elevator and service cores interrupted the rentable space – an acre a floor. The elevators provided an express service to observation decks and the glamorous Windows on the World restaurant; "local" elevators took 50,000 workers to their desks. (It was calculated that employees on higher floors spent a full working day a year just on rising to their tasks.) In the service cores, the power to cool a million refrigerators provided air-conditioning, a system managed, floor by floor, through 6,000 sensors.

The address, World Trade Center, was, in fact, that of a complex of seven buildings set in a five-acre plaza. It was a project of the Port of New York Authority, whose PATH rail link punched through the foundation walls, bringing commuters from New Jersey, many of them employed by the city agencies that occupied much of the space.

While the silhouettes of the Twin Towers became a New York icon, the majesty was in their height rather than in their architectural merit. The building that took over the title "world's tallest" in 1974, Chicago's Sears Tower, offered a great deal more visual panache.

Close to Madison Avenue, the new Ladies' Mile, the street of boutiques, a boutique skyscraper is squeezed into 57th Street (RIGHT). *It is the New York showcase for LVMH, the French luxury goods conglomerate. Just 60 ft. wide and 24 stories high, it presents to the street a folded façade of icy, hi-tech glass. Some critics welcomed it as "the new Art Deco," a breakthrough as significant as the Chrysler Building of the 1930s.*
CHRISTIAN DE PORTZAMPARC, 1999

December, 2004. Ground Zero has been cleared (ABOVE); *the last of almost 2 million tons of rubble has been barged to a reopened landfill on Staten Island. The Freedom Tower cornerstone, a 20-ton granite block quarried in upstate New York, is in place. A memorial, "Reflecting Absence," in the Towers' footprints will honor the dead of 9/11.*

No post-9/11 fear of heights for
Time Warner, the media group; and
with a budget of $1.7 billion, no
lack of confidence in the future of
tall buildings in New York. On the
site of the old Columbus Coliseum
exhibition halls, the Time Warner
Center rejuvenates a rundown area
(ABOVE). Behind its high curved
"podium," two towers rise 55
stories to 750 ft., in a complex
housing broadcasting studios, a
luxury hotel, theaters, restaurants,
shops, and apartments. For these,
the address is One Central Park –
worthy of the penthouse price tags
of up to $35 million. In
a lesson learned from 9/11, a
special system allows
communication between firefighters
and police in an emergency.
SKIDMORE, OWINGS &
MERRILL, 2004

The spire of the proposed Freedom
Tower at the World Trade Center
site (RIGHT) would top out at
1,776 ft. – the figures in the
nation's most significant date. Office
space would reach to the 70th floor,
then an open lattice structure would
house wind turbines that could
provide 20 percent of the building's
energy needs. The sides of the
building would be "torqued" to
deflect winds.
DAVID CHILDS

Index

Acknowledgments

Trawling through the 40 million archival photos held by Getty Images in collections like Archive in New York and Hulton in London is an enormous task even for the most skilled and conscientious of researchers. Adding 20 million additional archival images represented by Getty Images from Time & Life and the Museum of the City of New York makes managing the research for a book like this even more challenging. Ali Khoja has led all the research for *Building New York* with extraordinary assistance and cooperation from Kristeen Ballard who helped scour Getty for images from Lewis Hine, Berenice Abbott, Jacob Riis, and Ernst Haas whilst Michelle Franklin supplied often little known images from Margaret Bourke-White, Alfred Eisenstaedt, Alfred Stieglitz, and Walker Evans from her domain at Time & Life. Jill Reichenbach of the New York Historical Society and Tom Lisanti of the New York Public Library deserve special mention as does Sara Green, for her invaluable support. We would also like to thank Getty Images' Mitch Blank, Mark Porcelli, Mike Epp, Tea McAleer, Matt Green, and Liz Ihre and Time & Life's Jeff Burak and Arnold Horton who went well out of their way to deliver the goods once again.

CBM

AFP Agence France Presse, BC Byron Collection, DC Dahlstrom Collection, GEH George Eastman House, LC Library of Congress, MCNY Museum of the City of New York, TLP Time Life Pictures

t top, m middle, b bottom, l left, r right, all all

Non Getty Images Illustrations
12 Commissioners Plan, A Map of the City of New York, Collection of the New York Historical Society, #2081; 54-5 Picture Collection, The Branch Libraries, The New York Public Library, Astor, Lenox and Tilden Foundations #810063; 180b © Peter Aaron/Esto; 278-9b UN/DPI

All other illustrations are courtesy of Getty Images' special collections held by or represented by Getty Images. Those requiring further attribution are indicated as follows:

1 Lewis W. Hine/GEH; **2-3** Yale Joel/TLP; **16** Edwin Levick; **18-19, 20-1b, 21tl, 21tr** Talfor Holmes Pach/MCNY; **22** Wallace G. Levison/DC/TLP; **24** Lambert; **25, 26-7** Peter J. Eckel/TLP; **28b** BC/MCNY; **29t** Alfred Eisenstaedt/TLP; **29b** Edwin Levick; **31b** Yale Joel/TLP; **32tl** Peter J. Eckel/TLP; **34l** MCNY; **35** Edwin Levick; **36-7** MCNY; **38t** Ted Thai/TLP; **39** Keith Meyers/New York Times Co.; **40-1** BC/MCNY; **44, 45** Walker Evans/TLP; **46-7** MCNY; **48** Ed Clark/TLP; **49** Todd Webb; **51** John Craven;

52tl Wallace G. Levison/DC/TLP; **56-7** Edwin Levick; **57b** Mac Gramlich; **58** Margaret Bourke-White/TLP; **62-3** Arthur Schatz/TLP; **63tr** Carl Mydans/TLP; **66-7t** William England; **70** Wallace G. Levison/DC/TLP; **73tr** Jacob A. Riis/MCNY; **76, 78bl** Wallace G. Levison/DC/TLP; **78-9** BC/MCNY; **80l** Alfred Eisenstaedt/TLP; **80r** BC/MCNY; **82-3** Mario Tama; **83br** Melvin Levine/TLP; **84l** Ralph Morse; **84r, 85** Horace Abrahams; **86bl** Edwin Levick; **86-7** Henry Groskinsky/TLP; **88** all Alfred Eisenstaedt/TLP; **92lt** George B. Brainerd/DC/TLP; **92rb** Edwin Levick; **92lm, 92lb, 93, 94-5** Frederick Lewis; **98** BC/MCNY; **100** LC #3b24233; **101** Underwood & Underwood/GEH; **104, 105b** Wurts Bros./MCNY; **106, 108-9** all Arthur Gerlach/TLP; **110tr** Authenticated News; **110br** C.T. Brady, Jr.; **111t** P.L. Sperr; **111bl** BC/MCNY; **111br** Berenice Abbott/MCNY; **112** Lewis W. Hine/GEH; **113** Margaret Bourke-White/TLP; **116** Lewis W. Hine/GEH; **117** Oscar Graubner/TLP; **118-19** all Lewis W. Hine/GEH; **120bl** Bernard Hoffman/TLP; **120-1** George Enell; **122-3t, 123tr** Wurts Bros./MCNY; **124b** Wendell MacRae; **125** all Bernard Hoffman/TLP; **128tl** R. Gates; **128bl** Wurts Bros./MCNY; **128-9** Herbert Gehr/TLP; **130-1** all Ted Thai/TLP; **132t** William England; **132b** Yale Joel/TLP; **133** Hirz; **134-5** John Chiasson; **136-7** Berenice Abbott/MCNY; **137r** Slim Aarons; **138-9** Cornelis Verwaal/TLP; **139r** Mario Tama; **141tr** Frederick Lewis; **141bl** Edwin Levick; **141br** Martin Forstenzer; **142l, 143, 144bm, 144br, 145tr** MCNY; **148l** Joe Schilling/TLP; **148r** Al Fenn/TLP; **149** Lee Lockwood/TLP; **150l** Edwin Levick; **150r, 151** all Jerry Cooke; **152** all MCNY; **153b** Frederick Lewis; **154-5** all BC/MCNY; **156-7, 158t, 159** Frederick Lewis; **158b** BC/MCNY; **161t** Alfred Eisenstaedt/TLP; **161b** Ed Clark/TLP; **162-3** Wallace G. Levison/DC/TLP; **164, 164-5** George B. Brainerd/DC/TLP; **166-7** Dmitri Kessel/TLP; **168-9, 170, 171** Walker Evans/TLP; **173t** Al Fenn/TLP; **173br** Andreas Feininger/TLP; **174-5** Ted Thai/TLP; **177bl** Bernard Gotfryd; **177br**

Henry Groskinsky/TLP; **178** Bert Kopperl/Mansell/TLP; **181** William C. Shrout/TLP; **182-3** Arthur Swoger; **184l, 184-5** Bob Gomel/TLP; **186t** Alfred Eisenstaedt/TLP; **186b** Ted Hardin/TLP; **18** Ernst Haas; **188-9** Herbert Gehr/TLP; **189r** Mario Tama; **190tl** Timothy Hursley/AFP; **190bl** Don Emmert/AFP; **190-1** Mario Tama; **192** Ward Mountfortt, Jr.; **194-5** Carlo Bavagnoli/TLP; **196** all BC/MCNY; **197** Peter Kramer; **199** Graphic House; **202** Mario Tama; **204r** Eileen Darby/TLP; **206** Wallace G. Levison/DC/TLP; **207** Marie Hansen/TLP; **208** Edwin Levick; **209** Brent Stirton; **210br** Eliot Elisofon/TLP; **211t** Charles Peterson; **211m, 211b** MCNY; **212tl** Peter Stackpole/TLP; **212bl** Charles Peterson; **212-213t** Stephen Ferry; **215r** Donald Uhrbrock/TLP; **216t** Truman Moore/TLP; **217t** R. Gates; **216-17b** The Image Bank; **218-19t** Frederick Lewis; **218bl, 218-219b** National Baseball Hall of Fame Library/MLB Photos; **221** Frederick Lewis; **222, 223t** Ralph Morse/TLP; **223b** Roy Kemp; **227** Gjon Mili/TLP; **230-1** Alfred Stieglitz/GEH; **234-5, 236-7** Dmitri Kessel/TLP; **238tl** Atlas Photos; **238bl** Bill Pierce/TLP; **238-9** Atlas Photos; **240-1** Dmitri Kessel/TLP; **241tr** Peter L. Gould; **241br** Ted Russell/TLP; **242-3** Bob Gomel/TLP; **244-5** Melvin Levine/TLP; **246-7** Al Fenn/TLP; **248-9** Walter Sanders/TLP; **250l, 250-1** Andreas Feininger/TLP; **252-3t, 253b** Bernard Hoffman/TLP; **254-5** Horace Abrahams; **258-61** all Alfred Eisenstaedt/TLP; **262t** Blank Archives; **262b** Truman Moore/TLP; **266-7** Herbert Gehr/TLP; **267r** Alfred Eisenstaedt/TLP; **268** Tony Linck/TLP; **269** Bernard Levey/TLP; **270-1** Howard Sochurek/TLP; **272-3t, b** Grey Villet/TLP; **274-5** Dirck Halstead/TLP; **276** Henry Hammond; **279r** Peter J. Eckel/TLP; **280l** Lisa Larsen/TLP; **284-5** Schiff; **285r** Frank Scherschel/TLP; **288-9** Roy Kemp; **291** Adolph Studley; **292t, 292b** Ted Thai/TLP; **293** Ernst Haas; **295** Ted Thai/TLP; **296** Henry Groskinsky/TLP; **298** Mario Tama; **299** Doug Kanter/AFP; **300** Jean-Christian Bourcart; **301** Dbox courtesy of LMDC; **304bl** Edwin Levick; **304r** Melvin Levine/TLP

HOUSING THE IMAGES: THE LIBRARIES THAT SUPPLIED BUILDING NEW YORK

MUSEUM OF THE CITY OF NEW YORK, 1220 FIFTH AVENUE

GETTY IMAGES, ONE HUDSON STREET

TIME & LIFE, 1271 AVENUE OF THE AMERICAS